WHAT A "HO" CAN TEACH A WIFE

REAL TALK ABOUT CREATING YOUR
HOT, HOLY & HAPPY MARRIAGE

KARIN HAYSBERT

To the beautiful Queen daughters that God has blessed us with, Olivia and Octavia, and to Queens everywhere who know there's more. May you be filled with the overflowing love, joy, passion, and peace in marriage that you desire and that God intended. Here's to your hot, holy and happy marriages.

Praises for
"What A 'Ho' Can Teach A Wife"
and the Queen Wife

"My husband and I have been married for over 52 years. I highly recommend this marriage manual, "What a 'Ho' Can Teach A Wife" for engaged couples, newlyweds, middle-weds, and older-weds. It is full of wisdom, suggestions, and principles to help and support couples to enhance, heal, and enjoy their married life. I appreciate the self-disclosures of Karin's journey and the healing that she has experienced in herself and in her marriage. Thank God for her courage and obedience to God to write this book in order to help others in their marriages to receive fulfillment in all areas of their lives and relationships. I have received something to help me in my marriage of 52 years. You are never too old to learn something new. This is a must-read."

The Queen Mother
Pastor Delois Crosse
Delois Crosse Ministries

"What a 'Ho' Can Teach A Wife" by Karin Haysbert is straight FIRE! I love that the book is the truth from an experienced wife who has had real-life experiences in her marriage. Her transparency about living as a roommate with her husband for years and then learning to surrender to God to change her marriage is powerful. I truly enjoyed this chief Queen sharing her journey in this book, and I learned a thing or two. I recommend that every wife pick up this book if she wants to transform her marriage from any condition and take it to the next level."

Gail Crowder
Founder of The One Sexy Wife
Marriage and Life Coach, Speaker/Teacher, Author & Certified
Master Sexpert

"Karin is not only my sister and mentor but a courageous woman of God. When she told me about the idea for this book and the title, she was a bit anxious. Although she is candid, she can also be pretty reserved. But she is obedient to what God said: to write this book and 'shake the religious table,' which is inspiring in itself! The title can be jarring, but it's to get your attention. Otherwise, you might not be reading my words right now! This is a book that the church and the world needs. Divorce rates are high, and relationships are on life support because people aren't having REAL conversations and getting REAL help! We can learn a lot from Karin's experiences if we open up our hearts and minds. She uses biblical stories and spiritual truths to teach us all about keeping marriage hot, holy, and happy! I'm ready to learn so my future marriage can be on fire!"

Liris Crosse
Author of "Make the World Your Runway"
Supermodel, Motivational Speaker

***

"What I love about Karin is that she's not afraid to be honest about love & sex in marriage. I think that most women want to know they are not alone when it comes to these subjects. Don't be afraid to read this book and let it challenge to think differently about love and sex. We have to remember it's a gift from God for marriage, so open it up, and enjoy what God has given you Honey!"

Markita D. Collins
Best-Selling Author of "I'm Still Old Fashioned"
Certified Life Coach, Licensed Minister

"FREEDOM!!! That is the first word that comes to mind after reading this book. Karin takes you on a truth journey and forces you to dig deep and pull back every layer of hurt, assumption, and ignorance that has plagued your marriage...leaving you in a new optimal peace. Get ready to spread your legs and soar to new heights in intimacy!"

Kristin M. Young
Founder of Living the Vows and Fit & Sexy Wives

***

"Karin's passion for life, family, and her queenly status as God's daughter transcends common comprehension. As a woman of God and minister, she has a unique ability to listen deeply beyond what is being said, accentuating her gift to speak to your giant within. As a coach, Karin will bear your unresolved spiritual and emotional needs with intense compassion. She is skilled to help you discover your hidden desires and overcome your greatest challenges. I have known Karin for over 20 years and hail her as a voracious reader, a seeker of truth, and a dear friend. Karin is a true ambassador for Christ in love and deed, who unapologetically champions and celebrates the efficacy of women."

Nicole Davis
Co-Founder of Empower to Engage, Co-Author of "The Done Right Series":
Marriage Done Right Is Hard Work, But It's Worth It; Parenting Done Right Is Hard Work, But It's Worth It; Leadership Done Right Is Hard Work, But It's Worth It

"I'm excited and honored to endorse Karin Haysbert on the writing of her second book, "What A 'Ho' Can Teach A Wife." Her first book "Queen Arise," is power-packed with tools and nuggets, complete with her personal journey, experiences, and challenges. Karin is an avid reader who diligently applies the principles of God's Word to her everyday life and ministry. She is passionate about her assignment and her ministry to women of all socio-economic backgrounds. Through Karin's 'penned' voice, readers can discover and embrace their value and identity as God's beloved and priceless daughters. Karin equips the reader with the tools to dig deep and find and embrace the "Queen." In addition to her being a prolific writer, Karin is a much sought-after preacher and teacher of God's Word, as well as a dynamic motivational speaker."

Pastor Mary E. Buchanan
Ecclesia Ministries, International
Author of "The Apostolic Prophetic Midwife - The Call"

Table of Contents

Acknowledgments

Peace Queen Wives! First things first. Thank you, God, for allowing me to have lived and learned and to have come this far in my love and marriage. It's because of your grace that we still stand. Thank you!

Thank you to my loving husband, Brian. We are living in love together today in part because you wouldn't give up on us. Thank you for your undying commitment to working things out. You are kind and compassionate and a pillar of strength for our family. I love you with my whole heart and know that our journey will continue to get sweeter and sweeter. Smooches!

Thank you to my wonderful children, Malcolm, Olivia, and Octavia Haysbert. You have been there to see our marriage grow. I pray that we have taught you well and am excited for the loving families that you have (Malcom) and will have one day.

To my Mom and Dad, St. George and Delois Crosse, thank you for your love and your example!! Not many people have parents who have been married for over 50 years. I do! You have lived your vows and loved through it all. Thank you for the many lessons; I learned how to pray and stay together from you.

Many thanks to Fran and Walter Jones. You came into our lives at such a critical time. Thank you for your loving encouragement. Thank you for the classes you taught and the fellowships where authentic breakthroughs took place. Fran, thank you for helping to ground me and take me back to the most important thing: the two of us making our love work together.

Thank you for the Queen Wives and Sisters who have blessed my life and poured into my marriage: my grandmother, Lila Logan; my aunties, Lottie Artis and Charis Bowling; Nicole Davis; Markita Collins; Pastor Donna Scott; Kristin Young; Gail Crowder; and so many, many more. I love and appreciate you all.

Introduction

Why I wrote this book

Peace Queen! Welcome! I'm so glad you have picked up this book today. I put a lot of heart and soul into it from many years of joys and sorrows; blood, sweat and tears; laughter; and lots of good loving. Why did I write this book? I wrote it because there's a desire burning in me, and I think in you too.

Have you ever had a friend tell you about a movie she saw that was just so amazing? I mean she really hyped it up. It had an all-star cast. She gave you a snippet of the plot. Sounded interesting. She laughed until she cried. She really felt the story. You were sold. You couldn't wait to go. You grabbed your best girlfriend, stood in line, bought snacks, got seated in the crowded theater, watched it, and it turned out to be the biggest dud ever. What?!

I wrote this book because for so many of us, marriage has been the biggest dud or disappointment ever. Wait a minute! Where are all the butterflies and fun, romantic encounters, and wild sex all night long? This right here is not what I dreamed about. This can't be what God intended. No. Not at all. What happened? Marriage is supposed to be glorious! You mean I gave up my younger life and the freedom of singleness for this? Have you felt like that?

Let's clear something up right here and right now. God said in Proverbs 18:22, "When a man finds a wife, he finds a good thing, a treasure, and obtains favor from the Lord." When your husband put a ring on it, his life just went to another level. Even if it doesn't look like it yet, it did. He may not have realized it for one reason or another, but the favor of God was released in his life and in yours.

There are so many spiritual, emotional, and physical muscles that you and I get to strengthen and develop through the crucible of marriage. Yes, those difficult times are designed to make us bigger and better, stronger and wiser, happier and more abundant in our lives.

I wrote this book because I have talked to too many Queens who act indifferent about their almost sexless marriages because they crave physical intimacy and don't know how to re-establish their connections with their Kings. Marriage is the place where two people are meant to become one physically. The marriage bed was intended to be a place of great satisfaction, fulfillment, closeness, and climax. It is where we share with each other a part of us that no one else gets to have. It is sacred sexuality.

I wrote this book because so many couples don't feel like they're on the same page of life together. Marriage is the greatest place of power when you and your King walk together in harmony and unity.

I wrote this book because there are so many women who are hurting, bored, and lonely in their marriages. We are hurting in our marriages and from our marriages. I believe marriage is one of God's instruments for helping us to heal from the wounds of our past when we allow it to.

I wrote this book because so many Queens just don't understand men. Forget whether they understand us. Most don't. It's in marriage that we learn to master love, appreciation, and understanding of our Kings. If we do the work of marriage, we learn each other's language. We master how to communicate effectively. We are empowered to work together for success.

I wrote this book because I believe that forgiveness is often our biggest soul work in life. Doesn't marriage give us countless opportunities to forgive? It's in marriage that we truly grasp the depths of forgiveness and explore the vicissitudes of joy. We have the opportunity to grow and to understand as well as embrace what true bliss is in marriage.

I wrote this book because all of life points back to one thing: love. It's in marriage that we truly discover how to walk in love, day in and day out. Love is not just something that we show or do, it's who we are. We are love. When we allow the spirit of God to transform us, it transforms our lives together. Transformed marriages change our families. Changed families alter our communities. Altered communities revolutionize our world.

If we could all just allow more love into our lives, it changes everything. I believe that you probably feel just like me. There's more. More to life. More to love. More to you and to me. John 10:10 says that Jesus came "that we might have and enjoy life to the full until it overflows." He came to show us how to live the abundant, victorious life; to manifest that abundance is our birthright in every area of our lives. I believe that includes our marriages.

I think you're here because you believe that too, or you're at least willing to believe it. Am I right? You might be thinking that that's a really tall order. It sounds like marriage is the panacea of all things. Is it? No, but it can be the means through which God's love, which has the capacity to heal everything and everyone, can be expressed.

Are you ready, my dear Sisters? Let's do this thing! Let's start a revolution. The health and happiness of our marriages extend so far beyond us. We are literally impacting generations with the decisions we make in our relationships right now. Let's do our part in allowing the promises of God to be fulfilled in our lives and the world, simply by letting His glory reign in our hot, holy, happy marriages.

*"Happiness is always on the other side of being
teachable."*
Shannon L. Alder

How to use this book

Let me first remind you that YOU are the expert on your life.
I know that we have often been told or taught otherwise. We have
been made to believe that we don't know what's best and to not trust
ourselves. We've been conditioned to believe that we need to seek an
outside source for direction, with the idea that our answers are not
within us. Or maybe you've been taught not to trust anyone and to be
deeply suspicious of others.

Deep down inside, you probably know or at least sense many of
the ideas and concepts that I will share with you. Some things may
seem new to you. Other things will be shared in a new way with my
own special sauce on it. But, the real you—the Queen you, the Christ
you—knows. The wisdom of God is formed within you my Dear. I'm
merely helping you to access it.

With that said, Trust your gut. Lean on the voice of the Spirit of God
in you and be open to receive more. Here's the caveat. "Faith comes by
hearing," not from having heard. It is great that you may have heard
something before, but are you doing it? Just because you've heard
something, it doesn't mean that you know it. I always say that mental
assent is not knowledge. When you can live whatever ideal out, that's
when you really know it. There are many things in life that we must
hear over and over again. Repetition is the mother of learning. To know
something requires you to build your faith muscles continually.

Be open. When the carnal mind tries to rise up and tell you that
you already know something, ask yourself how you can apply it in a

new way. Where can you deepen your knowledge of the subject? How can you broaden your application? Ask the Spirit of God to show you what you haven't been seeing all along.

There are no coincidences. You have picked up this book on purpose. I would suggest that you read it all the way through once so that you can get a feel for the tone and tenor of the text. Find a beautiful journal book, which we will call our Queen Wife Journal, where you can write your thoughts down. Then, return to this book and read section by section. Answer the questions. Write down your insights. Be patient with yourself. Give yourself time and space to apply what you have learned or are seeing again.

Most of all, know that I am praying for you and with you. We are all Queen Wives on the journey to greater love and fulfillment in our marriages. I feel you because I am you. Your happiness is indeed on the other side of your being teachable, and it is in the midst of you trusting yourself, your King, and the God that lives freely in both of you.

A "Ho"? Really God?

A "Ho"? Really God? Why would you put me out there like that?" I had been wanting to write a book about being a wife for years. In fact, it was what I wanted to write about originally when God diverted me to create my first book, "Queen Arise: 40 Days to Liberating the Queen Within You." He told me in no uncertain terms, "No Daughter. Your cake is not quite fully baked yet. I still see batter in the pan. Work a little bit more on yourself. You change, develop and mature your marriage more. Then, you can write about marriage."

Of course, Daddy was right. I had to free the Queen within myself before I could become the Queen Wife that He was making me to be. I worked on myself. I studied and saw powerful things in the Word of God. I read plenty of books. I took courses, and I listened to other couples too. Let's face it, in this Information Age, we are not wanting for more advice. As things began to progress, I realized that it was time. I began to journal about marriage. In fact, my journal entry right before my 20th anniversary, "20 Things I Learned in 20 Years of Marriage," ended up being the basis of my first speaking engagement with wives and first course that I offered on marriage too. I was finally ready to write the book.

Now back to my original thought. I was reading the Word of God, a very familiar passage, where a lady of the evening, a harlot, or today some would call her a thot or a "Ho," was giving some real pearls of wisdom on how to deal with men. The funny thing is I remember hearing a message about this almost 25 years earlier. Now, with my newfound growth and awareness, I saw it in a new light. So many other revelations came forth from it. After I read the passages, the thought that arose within me, "Now ain't that what a 'Ho' teach a wife"?

It was in that split second that I heard the voice of God say, "That's the name of your next book." What? Are you for real? I heard a clear "Yes." Well, can I say that some time has elapsed since then? Like two years later?! Here we are! This is certainly not one of my most shining "Hear and obey" moments.

Why has it taken me awhile? Well, let's say I didn't want people to feel that I was condemning anyone, judging anyone, or putting anyone down. Truth be told, just about everybody's been a "Ho," according to someone's interpretation of Scriptures. Whether you have been with one person outside of marriage or many, or, even further, whether you had sex or just thought about doing it, some would say you have sinned.

I'm not here to get into a theological discussion. The bottom line is this. Everything the "Ho" is doing is not wrong. OK? It's just who she's doing it with that's problematic. I don't know about you, but if somebody can show me how to have greater fun, intimacy, and connection with my man, I want to at least hear about it.

That's not to say that I listen to just anybody, but people who are believers do not have the corner on all wisdom and knowledge. Yes. I said it. In fact, some of my favorite writers on the subject of marriage do not identify themselves as believers, at least not openly. Sometimes, people outside of religion can see things that we do not because they don't have all of the hang-ups that some people of faith have that we allow to stand in the way of our receiving truth. Don't believe me. Check this in Luke 16:8.

"And it is true that the children of this world are more shrewd in dealing with the world around them than are the children of the light."

Is that only talking about in this instance, in dealings with money and trade or simply in life? I think it can be both. Just saying.

Let's clear this up right here. If you're looking for an over-the-top, super-religious book, wrong book. I am pretty down-to-earth with things. I don't think anyone can ever accuse me of being "so heavenly minded that I am no earthly good" as I am today. I believe in sharing spiritual truths and practical tools to help you get to the marriage that you desire and God intended. I also like to share in a way that it can be a blessing to everyone. That's just how God uses me. If that's not your cup of tea, switch cups. I'll still love you.

Also, what I'll share with you about the "Ho" comes straight from the Word of God. 1 Corinthians 10:11 says that stories in Scripture are examples for us that we might gather counsel and advice from them. So, you can learn from the "Ho" just as much as you can learn from Mary the mother of Jesus. End of story.

Sometimes divorce is necessary

Another point. Let me put this out there right now. Although this book is about creating greater spiritual, emotional, and physical intimacy to save, support, and enrich your marriage, I do also believe that sometimes divorce is necessary. I believe that there are times when people need to go their separate ways. God is not into abuse. Just like many of you, I too have certain deal breakers.

As for divorce, the Scripture says that God hates it, but Moses allowed it. Jesus talks about it in Matthew 19:3, 8

"The Pharisees also came to Him (Jesus), testing Him, and saying to Him, 'Is it lawful for a man to divorce his wife for just any reason?'... He said to them, 'Moses, because of the hardness of your hearts, permitted you to divorce your wives, but from the beginning it was not so.'"

So basically, Jesus was saying that God never intended for a man and woman to divorce. Man was supposed to leave his parents and cleave to his wife. What this means is that he was supposed to be joined to his wife in every way. The two of you were to become one flesh. That's not just physically, that is also spiritually and emotionally. It is your job to join together so intimately that no man or woman can separate you.

So, why did Moses permit it? He did because of the hardness of people's hearts. Maybe there was unforgiveness. Maybe the couples were in circumstances that they couldn't overcome. Perhaps someone just decided that they didn't want to be married anymore. Let that Brother or Sister go. Real talk. Unless you are sure that God has spoken to you, you are not obligated to make anyone stay.

It is only by God's grace that I'm still married. Every single day,

I have to work on myself and my marriage. I'm not going to lie to you. It's work. I'm writing to you with over 22 years of marriage on the books (I have significant skin in the game). And, I've been married to one man for 22 years. I know plenty of people who've been married for over 20 years, but it's been to different people. No shade. It happens, and as I said, sometimes it should.

What I want you to know is that most of those 22 years were not very happy. Looking from the outside-in, I may have looked like I was happy, but I was not. I have to keep it real. I was just going day by day, living my life with my husband like roommates with occasional benefits, co-parenting our children. I write you as someone who felt so hopeless in my marriage. But, one day or rather over a period of time, things changed for me in a very drastic way as I changed. It's really a miracle. I'm here to tell you that things can turn around.

This book is for YOU if the following sound familiar:

- You've been married for a while and "The Thrill is Gone."
- You've been just existing in your marriage and not enjoying it.
- You're tired of hearing the old advice of you just need to love him and submit.
- You feel like... "Sex? What sex?"
- You've been going along to get along for so long and you're ready to get off of this merry-go-round.
- You're tired of fighting and never coming to any type of resolution.
- You're tired of not fighting and not addressing the concerns of your heart.
- You wish your King would step up and be the leader of your home.
- Most of all, you really love your husband, you want things to work, and you're willing to do the work.

If any of those reasons resonate with you, especially the last reason, you're in the right place at the right time for your marriage breakthrough. Are you ready? Let's go!

In the beginning

Just in case you aren't familiar with me, I thought I'd give you a little bit more of my background, where I came from, and where God has taken me and us. When I first got married, I was a young, single mother. I had just turned 29 and had dated my husband for a little over a year before we were engaged. I know some people don't believe in this, but I saw him first. He did end up "finding me," but I saw Brother Man first. I love to tell this story.

It was a hot summer day and I was attending our church's annual camp meeting. The ministry we belonged to was one of the megachurches in our town. Camp meeting was epic. Our church brought some of the biggest names in the Christian world every year. This year was no different.

Mike Murdock was teaching a day session. At the time, I was working for the school system and had the summers off. Glory! This gave me freedom to attend all of the day sessions. My husband was very involved in the church. He attended the church before I did and had been a member for many years. I knew who he was, but I didn't know him. He came from a pretty well-recognized family in Baltimore as do I.

So it happened that the two of us ended up in the same place at the same time. Mike Murdock had just taught a message on the "Uncommon Woman" taken from the text about Abigail. I will never forget that message. At the end of his powerful teaching, he called everyone to the altar who was believing God for an uncommon relationship. Check. That's me! I went to the altar, closed my eyes, and lifted my hands to receive a special impartation from God.

Mike Murdock was pacing back and forth in front of the line of us at the altar, and he began to get a word of knowledge. He said, "Some of you have been afraid to love, afraid to commit to a relationship. You've been afraid to get into a relationship because you didn't want to feel stuck. You didn't want to feel stuck in a relationship where you would not be able to get your physical needs met." Then he turned to someone near me (my husband) and said, "And that's you Brother, but the Holy Ghost knows what you want!" Next, I hear this person, a Brother beside me, yell out, "Hallelujah!" And fall to the floor next to my feet.

Well Queens, my interest was piqued to say the least. Who is this Brother who's at the church, during the day, probably in touch with God and wants a woman that can hook him up sideways on a regular? Hey! I take a peek down with my right eye to see who it was, and it was Brian. I always say that Brian fell at my feet (laughing out loud). Honestly, that's when he got on my radar. I thought to myself, "Let me check this Brother out a little bit more closely."

Long story short, we connected through the singles' ministry. I was the co-director, and he was one of the people I called on a regular basis to inform him about what events were taking place. I didn't ask to be assigned to his letter of the alphabet to make calls, The director gave the letter H list to me. I do think God hooked it up. Anyway, we were definitely friends first.

I was checking him out, but it took a while for him to see all of this fabulousness over here. We officially became an item within about seven months. A little over a year passed before he proposed. I didn't know that he was getting ready to propose. We had talked about marriage, but it did not look like he was getting ready to make a move. Brother Haysbert was about to get the left foot of "disfellowship" without a word from me. My sentiment was and is this: after a year, we're both grown, you ought to know if I'm the one or not and vice versa. If you don't know or I'm not, either way, I'm about to bounce. That's just me. You can do whatever you want to do, but there was no need to keep dating, in my opinion, unless the relationship is going

25

further towards marriage. Thankfully, he made a right choice and we made a good choice to be with each other. (Side note. My Single Queens, stop letting these Brothers waste your time and string you along endlessly. Set standards for yourself and keep those standards.)

Brian went to our parents and our pastor, got their blessings, and totally surprised me by proposing at one of our Singles Ministry "Light Club" events. You know, when the single people at church want to have the nightclub experience that they miss from when they used to go clubbing. They have a party, play contemporary gospel music, and call it a light club. Most of our church friends were there. I really was totally surprised, and it was beautiful.

Within four months, we were married. That, I would not recommend. (Another side note: Getting engaged is not just about planning your wedding; it is about planning your life together. It is also the time when you can change direction if you find that things are not going to work with the two of you. Be open. There's nothing wrong with breaking things off. It takes a lot of courage to get out of the train that you see is about to wreck.)

Although we both loved God and each other, there were many dynamics that we needed to discuss and should have hammered out before getting married. Brian wanted to get married right away. His family owned a catering business right across the street from our church, and they had a date in September. So, September it was. Lord have mercy.

I did mention to you that I was a single mother right? Starting a blended family has so many moving parts. You really do need proper counseling before you start one of them. We actually did go through counseling at our church. I'm sure that they did their best, but in hindsight, I can say we definitely needed a little more counseling for our situation. Nonetheless, we did what they told us to do, so we thought we were cool. Boy were we wrong.

Trouble in paradise

My husband, Brian, is a great guy. He's a man of God. He loves God and the Word. He's a prayer warrior. He's diligent and faithful, and has a servant's heart. I know that he says the same about me. The only problem is, that's not enough to make either of us excellent spouses.

Here's where problems came in. Trouble in paradise came quickly. I—like many young, on-fire-for-the-Lord people—thought that just because we both loved God then that would be all we needed and that the Holy Spirit would show us everything else. Ha! Wrong. Or at least, that was wrong for me. It's part of why I wrote this book.

My parents had been married for 30 years at the time of our wedding. My husband's parents had been married for almost 50 years. Sometimes, there is this assumption that because people are married a long time that it is a success. That's not always true. While both of our parents showed us longevity, they didn't always model the best practices for marriage. I'm sure that is true for most people.

I'll speak for myself. I saw a mom who did it all. She worked outside of the home, and when she got home, she clocked into her second full-time job. She did just about everything in the house too. She cooked. She cleaned. She handled the finances. My dad worked his job and pastored full time too, and when he came home, he just chilled, or at least that was my perception of what he was doing.

My impression of my parents' marriage was that Dad was in charge and Mom just went along with whatever he said. Besides, that is what my church culture taught us too. I had never seen them so much as have an argument. I remember one time growing up when my father raised his voice a little. That was the extent of it. To me, that was how you kept peace. You kept your mouth shut and went along to get along.

You were "submitted." The church and well-meaning people—some not so well-meaning—have jacked up submission royally. I was so afraid to do marriage wrong. I didn't want to seem like a failure. I kept my mouth shut, my head down, said nothing when I should have said something. For instance, I was told that a man doesn't want to feel like his wife is doing sexually with him what some other man taught her, and I swallowed that tale hook, line, and sinker. I failed to even challenge it. The big problem with that is if neither are virgins, then both of them got some tricks from somewhere else. OK? It was one of the many things that I allowed to keep me small and silenced in my marriage and in my life.

I was what I would call a "Christian Stepford Wife." Not quite as far as the Coming to America "whatever you like" with a bow, but certainly not an equal partner in marriage, or at least I didn't feel like one. It took a few years before I started to "rebel." Of course it wasn't rebellion, but based on the brainwashing I had been given, that's what it felt like initially.

I decided that I'm not sitting around here saying nothing. I have an opinion and I'm going to start to voice it. I'm going to stop ignoring things and acting like it's not happening. I was tired of feeling like I was walking around on eggshells. I was so miserable, but my pride wouldn't allow me to leave the marriage. Divorce was not something I was familiar with. And then there were three children involved. I had heard about all of the problems children of divorce experienced. I didn't want that to be what my children suffered through, so mostly, I suffered in silence with a few flare-ups of sharing my pain.

I felt lonely. I felt bored. I felt unappreciated. I felt like I had been duped. This was not what I signed up for. This was not the man that I married. I felt like Chris Rock. "Why Did I Get Married?" Now, this is not to say that Brian was just clicking his heels either, but he had no idea of the depth of my pain. I simply didn't share it with him. I just went on with life with a fake plastic smile on my face and a "God is good all the time" on repeat in my mouth, taking care of the home, taking care of our children, in some ways taking care of Brian, but certainly not taking care of myself or our marriage. This went on for years.

My awakening

Several years ago, I began to go through an awakening. We had our shares of ups and downs, mostly downs, but we're committed to at least staying married. The commitment was honestly due to our vows before God more than anything else. Also, as I mentioned, we had small children by then. I was homeschooling, and in some ways I felt really dependent on my husband because of that. I did not work or earn "my own money." I felt sort of trapped. Perhaps it was God, because if I had my own income, I might have left. I know this is something that keeps so many women in relationships that they shouldn't be in. I think it held me in this relationship so that I would stay, and it was a good thing. I felt stuck long enough to see the turnaround.

I'm a voracious reader and was trying to read Emerson Eggerichs's book, "Love and Respect." At the time, it was more than I could stomach. Respect? Ha! Respect him? In the introduction, he mentioned an author that I had heard of before. I knew I had some of his work. It was Dr. John Gottman. I love Dr. John Gottman. His work has done more to help me and my marriage than almost anyone else's. I'll share more on it later.

I began to devour his books and videos. There was one that struck me. He was sharing about how he was trying to market one of his books to a book executive. The gentleman was not that interested and wasn't hiding it. Finally, he cut Dr. Gottman off and asked, "Tell me one thing that anyone can do to change their marriage right now." Dr. Gottman paused for a moment and he said, "Honor your wife's dreams."

The book executive abruptly got up and left the office. Needless to say, Dr. Gottman was stunned. He thought, "Oh well. That didn't go well." What he didn't know then was that the gentleman got on the train and went straight home to his wife. The book executive's wife was surprised to see her husband home so early. What was her husband doing home at this time? Had he gotten fired?

He went straight to her and said, "I just have one question for you? What are your dreams?" She was shocked. Her heart melted and she replied, "I thought you'd never ask." They spent the rest of that evening opening their souls and intimately sharing with each other. It caused such a profound effect on their relationship. As you have probably guessed, Dr. Gottman got the book deal.

OK, that's a nice story Karin. What's the point? When I heard him tell that story, it stuck with me. I started to consider it. At this time, Brian and I were in a good place. The very next day, I walked into my husband's office and he turned to me and asked the same question, "What are your dreams?" I was dumbfounded. I realized that the sad part was that I had no response. I said, "I have to get back to you." This began my awakening.

I realized that I had become numb and unconscious to life itself. I was caught up in living the life that everyone else said I was supposed to live. I could lead worship. I could sing. I could shout. I could teach. I could pray. I could run around and do everything everyone else wanted, but I could not tell you exactly what God called me to do right now besides being a wife and mother. Beyond that, I couldn't tell you what I wanted. That is not to disparage those roles in the least. I simply realized that I wasn't holding myself to any standard of Zoe life, the God kind of life, the divine life of more that God was calling me into because of my own fears and unconsciousness. That wasn't anyone else's responsibility. That isn't the church or society's fault. My life is my responsibility. I woke up!

Divine life and God's promises

Slowly but surely, I began to change. People who saw me would not have thought that I was the way that I was. They had no idea how constricted and confined I felt. And, it was really my doing. I couldn't even say it was Brian. I believe that we go through trials and overcome so that we can help others to do the same. It was ordained for me to go through that spiritual, emotional, and mental imprisonment so that I could minister liberation to others as I continually am freed.

John 10:10 says that Jesus came that we might have an enjoy life to the full until it overflows. He came to show us how to do it. I wanted that life. For once, I was demanding it for myself. It didn't happen all at once, and it's still in process, but I began to get clear about my own desires. To own them. I decided that I would openly express myself. I was going have the life God promised.

It became my quest, and I made it unapologetically. I decided to be happily married. I committed to be an excellent wife in a happy marriage. Now, here's the other part: with or without Brian. I had to get to the point where I could accept my greatest fear.

If it all fell apart, if my marriage ended, what was I afraid of? Could I support myself? Of course, I have many marketable skills. Would my children be OK? That's another Yes. They are pretty mature. Spending all of their lives being homeschooled with me meant that we had many discussions. I taught them everything I learned. I taught them how to love God and how to depend on Him fully. I taught them to be strong and to think for themselves. I taught them how to be responsible. I admire the wisdom that they have. Would I feel like a failure? Maybe. Would that matter? No. I became determined to do everything that I could do so that if things didn't work, I could say that I gave it my all. I was driven for one thing: the hot, holy, happy marriage.

Hot, Holy, Happy!

Let me explain this adventure that we are embarking on together. It's broken into three parts. First, the hotness. Just in case you have forgotten. God created sex. It's supposed to bring us the greatest pleasure in the context of marriage. Our marriages are designed to be hot, passionate, and full of sizzle. If your marriage is lacking in this area, so was mine. I'll share some things that helped to turn things around for us.

Secondly, the holiness. Your intimacy must extend beyond the physical and into the spiritual and emotional. There is a oneness that can only be described as sacred in marriage. In this section, we'll discuss how to develop spiritual oneness as being on one accord. If this has been your Achilles' heel, join the club. We struggled with that too. I have some ideas that can support you in this.

And lastly, the happiness. I don't know about you, but if I'm not going to be happy, then what's the point? Do you really think God intended for us to be miserable all of our lives in a marriage? Your purpose is to bring forth the glory of God in your life. It is to demonstrate his love and light to a world of darkness. We should be the happiest people on the planet. Sadly, we often are not. In this section, I will share what I have used to get to my happy place in marriage. Perfect? Not at all, but I am happy and you can be too. After spending too many years unhappy, it's glorious to feel really at peace and enjoy my life and my marriage.

So Queen, I'll share some things that you've heard. I may share a few things that you haven't, but if you're reading this book, let's trust that God wanted you to hear something of value for yourself and for your marriage. If you find one great key that unlocks more intimacy for you in your union, I'd say it's worth it. Here's my big ask. It's something that I tell my mentoring clients often.

Keep an open mind and heart. Again, instead of saying, "I already know that," why not ask instead, "How can I go deeper with this?" Rather than saying, "That won't work for me," how about asking, "How can this work for me?" You may have heard it before, but you didn't hear it from me or in my way. Furthermore, I'll repeat, faith comes by hearing and not from having heard. Let's focus on what we can do with our knowledge. In short, humility will allow you to get the most out of this and any other journey of faith. I say faith because building greater intimacy in your marriage will place a demand on your faith like never before.

If you haven't gotten it already, I also invite you to have your Queen Wife Journal. In it, write down things that jump out at you. Write down your questions. You can e-mail me your questions at support@queensforchrist.org. Or you can join my Facebook Group for this book at www.hotholyhappy.com. If you're brave, I know that you are, share your questions or insights there. You never know how many other Queens have the same question or will benefit from your sharing. We are all in this together.

Throughout the book, I will ask you to ask yourself lots of questions. I include lots of tips and tricks to help you throughout the book and in designated sections. Date and write the answers to questions and whatever comes up for you in your Queen Wife Journal. It's great to reflect and lay out your divine strategy. It's also a blessing to be able to go back in time and see where God has brought you from. Queen, you are about to build a sho'nuff marriage testimony.

My disclaimer

Here's my disclaimer. I am not a doctor or therapist, although I mentor and coach women and wives through my Queen Wife

Mastery Membership Program and programs on spiritual and personal empowerment and development. These are my ideas based on what I have experienced in over 20 years of marriage as well as what I have researched, learned, and observed in others. Some things will work for you while others may have to put on the shelf or put aside. It's a-OK. I'm just the messenger. It's your marriage. Pray. Ask God to direct you. Follow Him above all else. God will show you how to apply things with wisdom.

For more info on Queen Wife Mastery Membership Program and my other empowerment programs, go to www.teachawife.com.

Are you ready to have the hot, holy, happy marriage that you desire, deserve, and that God intended? Let's go. Wife School is in session.

PART ONE:
The Hotness

What a "Ho" Can Teach A Wife

CHAPTER 1

I'm Here for You

Peace Queen!

Let's start right here with the hotness. Unless you had an arranged marriage, which might not have been a bad idea… hmmmm, you probably had some kind of initial attraction to your King. OK. I know there are those of you who may have been attracted to his beautiful spirit and mind first and his behind second, but I digress. There may be some of you who really couldn't stand him in the beginning. Then, there may even be a few Queens who just said, "What the heck, I have no other prospects. I'll just go with him." By the way, that's often disastrous. For most people, there is some type of attraction—often including a physical attraction—that first piqued your interest. Now, if you are one of the few who that doesn't matter to at all, thank you for helping to round out the human race. For the rest of us, there needs to be some fire. That's why I'm talking about the hotness first.

This book is primarily for wives, but I know that Queens who want to be wives will read it too. Let me take a little bunny trail and talk to you all for a moment. You might be thinking, "But Karin, [let me rephrase that] Minister Karin, shouldn't we first be looking at whether he's saved and sanctified and going to be caught up to meet Jesus when He comes back? I thought our focus should first be whether or not we are unequally yoked spiritually."

Well, that is a valid point. Let's be real. You wanted real talk right? You must have chemistry. What you don't want is to have to force yourself to make love to anybody because there is no physical attraction. Real talk. Yes, you want a godly man, but physical attraction is important.

*"Leah was tender eyed; but Rachel was beautiful and well
favoured."*

Genesis 29:17

Remember Jacob. He spent seven years working for Laban so that
he could have his daughter, Rachel, as his wife. He was madly in love
with her. Think about it. Seven years! I wonder if my husband would
have worked that long to get me. Hmmm.

Then, on his wedding night, Laban did a switch-a-roo. He brought
Leah to Jacob under the cover of nightfall as if he is giving him his
desired bride Rachel. The Scripture says she was weak-eyed or tender-
eyed. I've heard some suggest that she may have been cross-eyed.
Whatever that meant, she was just not as vibrant and beautiful as her
younger sister as a result of it.

How did Jacob not know that he wasn't with Rachel? Leah must have
been totally covered and must not have said a word all night. I know
Jacob had to have known what Rachel's voice sounded like. He could've
been really drunk. You know they really drank at those wedding feasts.
Check Jesus's first miracle in John 2. They drank so much wine that Jesus
had to turn some water into more wine. I'm just saying.

So Jacob gets to the wedding night, ready to wear a Sister out,
thinks he has just made love to the love of his life and finds out it's
Leah and not Rachel? Now he's stuck with this wife he doesn't want
because in order to get the woman he wants, he has to endure the
wife that he doesn't. On top of that, he had to work for Laban seven
more years to get Rachel. Tragic!

That's some low-level stuff that Laban did, but Jacob wasn't all
that squeaky clean himself. Sometimes we reap what we sow, but I

digress. The point of my sharing that aspect of the story is that if you don't have chemistry with someone, my advice would be to move on. No one wants to feel stuck with someone who they don't want. It's not fair to anyone. There is someone for everyone. There is a King who will love you and desire you just the way you are and vice versa.

Sure, physical chemistry is not the only thing that's important. I know that you may have to give someone a chance initially. I think you should pray and seek God's wisdom, but after some time, if your desire for a Brother doesn't seem to grow and increase, get to stepping. Move on!

I always say that there are 7 billion, with a "b," people in this world. God is a God of abundance. There is no reason why you should settle for anything less than His best for you. Married or single. OK. Now that I've gotten that off of my chest. I hope you get why I'm talking about sexual chemistry and intimacy first.

"There are two things we often feel like shouldn't be talked about in church, and we want a lot of both of them—money and sex."
Karin Haysbert

Let's talk about sex baby!

You haven't been saved all your life. You know you remember that song by Salt-N-Pepa. Let's talk about it. There are two things we are often told or feel like we shouldn't talk about in church. The funny thing is that we want a lot of both of them. They are money and sex. If you don't want a lot of both of them, I'm wondering what's going on with you. The overflowing life means that you always have more than enough. If I just have enough for me financially, how can I be a blessing to the lives of others? How can I fulfill my mission in the Earth with just enough? We were wired for abundance.

Additionally, in marriage, if you're getting just enough sex or not enough sexual intimacy, something's wrong. Really wrong. Before we dive into all the do's of sex, let's establish a foundation for sexual intimacy and bust up some of the don'ts. I want to blast some of the sexual myths that have been plaguing the minds of believers like forever. This might not be for you. It might be for your cousin, so read on.

"Our souls crave intimacy."
Erwin Raphael McManus

Real sexual intimacy

Before we go into sexual intimacy, let's just talk about the word intimacy itself. Intimacy is having close, loving relations. It involves familiarity or friendship. It is when you mingle your lives together. There is an openness and vulnerability that allows each other to be seen. Intimacy means "Into-Me-See." Real sexual intimacy is built on the foundation of spiritual and emotional intimacy. It is shallow and not as meaningful when we base our sexual intimacy on anything less or purely from a physical basis. Hang tight. We will tap into the various aspects of intimacy throughout the book.

"Your real sexual intimacy is an expression of the temperature of your inner lives together."

It's true. Your real sexual intimacy is an expression of the temperature of your inner lives together. That is why it is often said that the level of your sexual intimacy is a barometer of the health of your overall relationship. When we feel close to our Kings and there is mutual love, appreciation, and respect, it leads to greater sweetness and satisfaction in the bedroom. You want to please each other, meeting each other's needs in every way.

In Dr. Willard Harley Jr.'s book, "His Needs, Her Needs: Building an Affair-Proof Marriage," he shares the top needs between men and women in marriage. For most men, sexual fulfillment is at the top of the list. He states, "The typical wife doesn't understand her husband's deep need for sex any more than the typical husband understands his wife's deep need for affection." Of course these are generalizations, and there are exceptions, but men generally speaking—at least earlier in life—have a tendency to have a much higher need for sex. This is not just a want; it is a need. Men have as much as 30 times the amount of testosterone in their bodies than women do, which is why they often have a much higher sex drive. Testosterone is the hormone that drives our sexual desire. Around the age of 30, those levels will start to gradually decline in men.

"...and the two shall become one flesh..."
Mark 10:8

What I want you to gather from this is the different approach that each of us takes. Men have a driving need for sex. As we fulfill that beautiful desire together, it allows them to feel closer to us or more intimate with us. We, however, have as strong a need for affection. We want to feel loved and cared for. We desire to feel protected and approved of. We thrive on non-sexual touch and affection. That's not to say that we don't want to get it on. We most certainly do! The difference is that our desire to make love is often preceded by feelings of closeness and intimacy. When our hearts are honored and we feel loved, it makes it so easy to offer our bodies to our Kings. Sometimes, it seems like God just has some kind of sense of humor, because somebody is going to have to act in love in order to make this work. Will it be you? Will you step up? Let's examine your feelings about your sexual intimacy.

Grab your Queen Wife Journal.

I want you to answer these questions on a scale of 1 to 10, 1 being "Chile please!" and 10 being "I'm caught up in the rapture of love." Don't think long about it. Write the first number that pops in your head.

- How's your sexual intimacy?
- Is it what you want it to be?
- Do you feel free to express yourself sexually with your husband?
- Is there an openness and a playfulness in your marital bed?
- Do you make love as often as you would like to?
- Overall, are you sexually satisfied?
- Do you have orgasms as much as you would like?
- If so, are your orgasms as intense as you would like them to be?
- Have you taken your King for granted in this area?
- Do you feel taken for granted in your marriage bed?
- Would you like your sex life to be better?

After you answered all of these questions, observe what numbers stand out the most. Does it reveal that you are pretty happy with your sexual intimacy? Are you lukewarm about it? Or is it like the frozen tundra? Write down any thoughts or feelings that come up from taking a closer look and how you feel about it.

When sexual intimacy is hard

Sometimes being sexually intimate with your husband is just hard. It may have started out with a blaze of glory but then it cooled. Perhaps you came together as young lovers but things changed as soon as you became parents. The pressures of life piled on and your intimate encounters took a nosedive. Or maybe you both are just dealing with ghosts of the past. Is sexual shame or guilt holding back the floodgates of pleasure for one or both of you? Here's the truth. We all come into relationships with plenty of baggage. There's a lot of history between the two of you. Often that history is with other people sexually. Sometimes there's been abuse in your past. You may have even been sexually violated. Or, it could just be that sex was never great between the two of you. You tried. It didn't work. You gave up. These things will affect you. And you will need to be open, honest, and willing to deal with it.

If your sexual intimacy has been difficult, why has it been so? What is your part in this? No one person is usually at fault, but you both are responsible for how it has ended up. Take an honest assessment of yourself in this. If sexual intimacy has been hard for you, why do you think that is?

Unshackled sexuality

I understand very intimately how your sexual past can affect your sexual intimacy. In my book "Queen Arise," I shared a very private part of my life publicly. As I said earlier, this was the book that God changed my plans of writing. The entries in "Queen Arise" are from my private journal. They are my private conversations with God that I never thought would be open to y'all.

One of my transformations had to do with facing the sexual violations that occurred to me when I was a child. Did you know that according to the National Center for Victims of Crime, 1 in 5 girls is a victim of child sexual abuse? Most often, it is not "Eddie Lester the Child Molester" hanging in the bushes at the playground. It is someone that they know and usually trust.

That's what happened to me. I had no idea of how my interpretation of those events placed shackles on my own sexuality. Sometimes we want to simply brush these old experiences off and say, "It's under the blood of Jesus," but you might need to actually sit down and talk with someone about it if you are having challenges with your sexual intimacy today. There may be a need for you to unpack it, really face it, and deal with it so that you can be free to enjoy sexual oneness and satisfaction like God intended. With that said, I'd like to share this excerpt from my first book. I trust that it will bless you. ...

"Making love! Doing it! SEX!! We all want it, well most of us do. We all NEED it; now, that's true. We're all here because of it. OK, we can all agree on that— lol. Suffice it to say, it is a central part of who we are. But somehow sex for me had become sullied, dirty, shameful, and painful.

'I have been delivered!' 'From what?' 'None of your business! That's between God and me. Some things should go with you to the grave,' he said.

That's what my pastor told us that we should say. What he was really telling us is that we should hide our pain, conceal our struggles, and never asked for help. Fake it till you make it. That's how I heard it.

'You're a leader. What are you doing at the altar?' he chided. I heard, 'You better not show yourself. Nobody needs to know about you and your business. Not even your spouse.'

What I didn't know, was that these were the words of a wounded man who wanted to hide himself. He was living more than a double life and because of

44

my own shame, I swallowed it all, hook line and sinker. I swallowed my shame. I swallowed my fear. I swallowed the feeling that I was "damaged goods" and that if anyone really knew my story, they wouldn't accept me. No one would really want me…

So here I was, pretending the pain did not exist. I put on my 'Praise the Lords.' I looked holy, righteous, sanctified, and whole.

When the flower is forced to open its petals before the appointed time, there will be consequences, often-negative consequences.

Flashback! When an older "family member" introduced me to a 'fun game that would feel really good', I was in. Besides, he was like a big brother to me. I was a lonely, only child and I looked up to him. It didn't involve intercourse. It was a 'humping game' fully clothed, but sometimes not. A desire was awakened. And since it was a game, and it was fun, I told other people about it in my naïveté. It was just a part of my summer fun, or so I thought.

The next summer, when I saw my 'big brother' again, I was ready for the game. But he was not. What I didn't know was that from one year to the next, it seems that he had gone to the next level in the game, the next world. He was much more interested in carrying out the next level game with a cousin of mine. This cousin was light-skinned, with light eyes, and long hair. I felt so rejected, not good enough, and not pretty enough. I didn't realize it then, but God was protecting me.

What I saw as rejection was really protection.

I thought I was rejected because I was darker, had short hair, and those 'big bubba lips', the phrase bullies used to tease me with. I thought I was not beautiful. That's why he doesn't want to play the game with me! From then on, the lively, gregarious, little girl retreated. I became quiet, I became shy and low self-esteem became a dangling noose around my neck. I couldn't get too far from it or it would choke me and pull me back.

At the same time, we moved back to Baltimore from the DC area, where my father began a new job and took on another church assignment. In DC, he at least spent some time with me but in Baltimore, all he did was work. I withdrew more. My mom never seemed to connect with me on an emotional level. I shrank more. My parents had another child and she got all of the attention. I sank even deeper into the pain, reeling in the rejection.

I've always been a reader. Going through my dad's library, I came across some old medical journals. I saw a picture of a young girl who was pregnant! Oh my God, could I be pregnant? I was ignorant of the facts of life. Fear gripped me. I went to the library and researched more. OH! I'm not pregnant, but I am still damaged, dirty. SHAME entered my heart. I should have never done this "humping game." It's not a game at all. It's my fault. I played this game and told others about it too. I'm a terrible person. That is how I felt.

Then, over the years, sex became the forbidden fruit that everyone wants but you are not supposed to have… that is, unless you are married. Well, I wasn't married and I had sex. I had sex to feel loved. I had sex to feel wanted. I had sex to have a boyfriend. I didn't do it much, but enough to swim in the shame.

Time passed. I began to see sex as a gift. It's a gift I wanted to share with my future spouse, but I still pushed the boundaries from time to time. Sex is something that you should never have to say 'No' to, but when you skirt the edges after making a decision to wait, you can make your body say 'No' to what it's designed to say 'Yes' to. That is called 'Playing with fire.' You will get burned! Then we get married, we think we'll automatically say 'Yes.' It didn't happen that way for me.

I was so bound by my past shame and guilt and enslaved by the 'submission' omissions, you know the stuff that folk left out of the story of submission, that for almost two decades, I waited for my husband to give me permission to be free sexually. He couldn't. It was only mine to give.

So, I gave myself permission through forgiveness. I forgave myself for every sexual mistake because I know that it was a deeper issue. It was shame. It was guilt. It was fear of rejection. It was fear of being unlovable. It was fear of never being loved. I forgave everyone who violated me and for my violation of others. I forgave myself for what I did knowingly and for that which was done without knowledge. I realize that the past is over and I refused to allow it to tie me to a grindstone of guilt.

I decided to live my life unshackled. I gave myself the freedom to explore the heights of pleasure and the depths of desire. It is God's gift to me. It's my gift to myself… to be free…really free in unshackled sexuality."

Excerpt from "Queen Arise: 40 Days to Liberating the Queen Within You"

To get your copy of "Queen Arise" in the US, go to www.queenarisebook. com. Outside of the US, grab your copy on Amazon at bit.ly/queenarise40.

There's so much that could be unpacked from that entry. Could you see yourself anywhere in that passage? Did it make you think of a struggle you have had or do have? I must say this. If you are having trouble working through pain from your sexual past, please seek out a mentor to assist you. Or for very deep issues, seek a qualified therapist or counselor. There is no shame in asking for or getting help.

Grab your Queen Wife Journal.

Review each section offered in this chapter. What did you learn? What did you see in a new way? Where do you need to grow? Take your Queen Wife Journal and put a strategy together.

Here's what I want you to know Queen, God wants you to be free. Free to love yourself. Free to love your body. Free to experience the deep pleasures that your body holds. Free to be totally open and vulnerable with your King. As we delve into sexual intimacy, I want to start with the most important person that you must be intimate with: yourself.

CHAPTER 2

Intimacy with Yourself

"Oh yes, you shaped me first inside, then out;
you formed me in my mother's womb.
I thank you, High God—you're breathtaking!
Body and soul, I am marvelously made!
I worship in adoration—what a creation!
You know me inside and out,
you know every bone in my body;
You know exactly how I was made, bit by bit,
how I was sculpted from nothing into something.
Like an open book, you watched me grow from conception to birth;
all the stages of my life were spread out before you,
The days of my life all prepared
before I'd even lived one day."
Psalms 139:14-16

May I suggest something to you? We can only be totally intimate with our husbands when we've been totally intimate with ourselves. I'm not talking about self-pleasuring, although that's great too, but I'm talking about being totally open and honest with yourself about yourself. Do you know yourself? Have you looked into the deep recesses of your soul and seen how absolutely breathtaking you are? Can you acknowledge how marvelously made you are?

God knows you inside and out and sees you as utter perfection. Do you? Warts and all. Cellulite and all the love handles you can handle, God still sees you as very good. What do you see when you look inside and outside of yourself?

Before I could improve my intimacy with my husband, I had to address developing greater intimacy with myself. I had to get real with myself about how I was approaching my own sense of self as it pertained to my sexuality. I had to unpack some of the sexual baggage and pain that I was walking around in like a pair of worn-out shoes that are too small and were never beautiful on me in the first place. I became willing to look at the feelings and desires that I had not only suppressed but also repressed.

There are some things that I was suppressing, and I was conscious of them like I'm not in charge of my own pleasure. I'm dependent on my husband to be sexually aware and alive. Then, there were things that I was repressing, meaning I was not even aware that I was doing it. Unknown to me, I carried so much shame about the sexual molestation. It had fractured my soul. I felt unclean and undeserving of pleasure now. I felt like my innocence was taken from me but not entirely against my will because it was presented as a game, which actually was pleasurable. How could I let that happen? Of course I realize now that these feelings were unfounded, but you have to remember the house that I grew up in. The culture of church that places so much shame on sexuality in general and on premarital sexual contact in particular. Feelings of not being good enough, like damaged goods, and unworthy were all around me. I had to examine those stories and many others that I was telling myself about what had happened to me and what those stories meant. I became vigilant about confronting some of the beliefs that I picked up about sexuality as a whole. I was willing to ask myself if I believed they were true and why. I invite you to do the same.

I have found that nothing can stop a woman who has a made-up mind. My mind was made up. I wanted to see myself as the sensual, sexual being that God created me as. In order to do that, I had to begin to adore every part of my body from the tip of the longest hair on my head down to the soles of my beautiful feet, and I've got some fly feet. I had to love every part of myself inside and outside, and express love and gratitude to every part of myself. I allowed myself to take the time to nurture my body and to treat it like the glorious temple that it is. This may not sound like it has anything to do with sexual intimacy. I promise you that it does. When you see your temple as sacred, beautiful, and worthy of pleasure, it opens you up to receive that.

Your pleasure is in your hands

Pleasure. Where are you with pleasure in your life, and I am not just talking about sexual satisfaction? You hold the key to your pleasure and desire. You are responsible for that. Have you given that task to someone else? If you have, you have released your own power for pleasure.

How can you take your power back in this area? I encourage you to explore your body with and without your husband. How can you tell him what feels good if you don't know what feels good. Most people don't even know their own bodies and yet want their spouses to know their body enough to please them. Every woman is unique. What your husband experienced in the past, saw on movies or videos, or even heard the Brothers talked about in the locker room may not entirely apply to you. First, people in the movies and videos are acting. Even though art can imitate life, sometimes it's just pure fiction. We forget that. Secondly, most of those Brothers in the locker room are lying. Sorry Kings.

There are many sexual organs in a woman's body that are part of our pleasure map. Many of which are rarely talked about. We'll get to that later. Right now, I want to deal with your largest sexual organ.

It's not your vagina or your vulva or your clitoris or G-spot or A-spot. It's that organ between your two ears. Your brain. Let's clear up a few myths that are insane on the membrane for us Queens and especially for women of faith.

You know that's a lie:
Sexual myths some church folks believe

Sex is private and something that should be discussed only between the couple.

Sometimes people feel like we shouldn't talk about sex because it should be private. Sex is something you need to keep between the two of you. "How dare you talk about such discreet things so indiscreetly, especially in the house of God," some people think.

Although every couple needs to talk about sex with one another frequently and more than with anyone else, sex is something that should be handled in our spiritual communities. If God talks about sexuality, and He does, the church should be talking about it too.

I believe these talks need to go far beyond reasons why we should refrain from premarital sex or fornication and adultery. In some cases, we haven't even been told reasons. We've just been told don't do it because the Bible says so. Ummm, Sir, that is not enough. We must stop acting like we were born on pews and spent our whole lives there, never making a mistake. We need to tell our Brothers and Sisters about the effects of sex outside of marriage too. We need to talk about the emotional impact. We need to tell the truth about the differences between men and women and how we process it; also we need to talk about why it's a good idea to keep your garden closed. We need to say more than the, "You should only have sex with your husband or wife," talks. Duh! We need to be really straight up with spouses, male and female, who are withholding sexual intimacy from their partners and how they are putting their partners at risk. Everyone is responsible for their own actions, but are you a contributing factor to your spouse stepping out.

I think we should be having real sexual education talks in the church. Marriage Ministries, wake up. If we are not able to handle the subject, then we need to bring people from the outside in to teach it. Sex is an integral part of our married lives. It needs to be shared in an authentic way and openly.

Sex is more about being fruitful and multiplying.

Then, there are the people who want to make sex only or mostly about procreation. This is totally laughable. I contend that sex is not just for our procreation; it is mostly for our recreation and connection. When God gave the command for us to be fruitful and to multiply, He knew what He was doing. God made sex fun and pleasurable so that you would want to do it all the time. He even packed immense benefits in making love. We will talk more about that later too. Trust that He knows what He's doing.

When you get married, sex just happens naturally.

Why we think that sex will just happen naturally just because we said "I do" is a bit of a fairytale in addition to a myth. I think we've seen too many fantasies on the Silver Screen. Now you know that's a lie. Just because a key can fit into a lock, that doesn't mean you know how to turn it. Sex does not just happen naturally any more than you having a great marriage happens naturally. I don't care how holy you are, you can be as pure as the un-driven snow, but if you don't get some wisdom, knowledge, and understanding about yourself, each other's bodies, what you find pleasurable, and what your spouse enjoys too, you're probably not going to have great sex. Nothing just comes naturally in marriage. Great sexual intimacy is no exception. Let me put the emphasis on great sex. Yes, you may know naturally that penis fits into vagina, but that does not make great sex alone.

Usually the husband has a high sex drive, and the wife has to endure it.

Lord Jesus, this one burns me up. While this may be true earlier in marriage for some, when your husband's testosterone levels are much higher, it's not always true with everyone, and it doesn't always stay true even if it was at one point.

I have talked to plenty of women who want sex more than their husbands do for a variety of reasons. Not only are there Queens who have greater appetites for sex than their Kings, but the myth that we just have to endure it boggles my mind. I don't know about you, but it turns me on to have my husband desire me. I want it just as much as he does and sometimes a whole lot more.

In women, our sexual peak seems to come later. I believe that sometimes it has to do with our maturing and becoming more comfortable in our skin. God has a funny sense of humor. Our sexual desire can often be peaking when theirs may be waning. This is where agape love comes into play, and you must seek to love and serve each other's needs.

Whoever has the lowest sexual drive should determine sexual frequency in marriage.

Myth! Who should determine how often a couple makes love? The one who wants it more or the one who wants it less? For example, if you want to make love three times a week and he wants to make love three times a month, you should just submit and deal with it. Really! 1 Corinthians 7 speaks to the contrary.

This passage states that as husband and wife, you willingly yield your bodies to one another. You must find a meeting ground. Facts! One spouse shouldn't be hot and bothered and not satisfied. Although this does not justify any infidelity by any means, it can put the unsatisfied spouse at risk. This is what agape love is all about. It is unselfish love. It's up to each partner to work on themselves and with each other to find a joyful, sexy medium.

Sex should be spontaneous, not planned.

Who says that sex should be spontaneous alone? Sex should just be. As busy and hectic as our lives are, if we're waiting for it to happen spontaneously, there are always 10 to 20 unfinished things on our "to do" lists that can take precedence, especially for us wives who handle the majority of life at home.

While spontaneous sex may be exciting, planned sex can be too. In fact, the planned rendezvous can be more exciting. You've had time to stoke the fires of your desire. You've been marinating on the thought of breaking his back all day. Your King has put effort into wooing you and setting the stage for your lovemaking. By the time you come together, you are red-hot and ready to go. Both can be equally as rewarding.

Here's a tip. If you do not plan your intimate moments, try planning some of them. You probably need to have way more sex than you're having any way. You can't base it only on whether or not you feel like making love. I don't always feel like working out, but I do it anyway because I know it's the best thing for my body. The same is true with sex. It does a body good. It does a mind good. It does a heart good. It does your marriage good.

Developing your sexual intimacy with yourself

Now that we've cleared up a few of the many myths floating around, let's get down to the nitty-gritty. Your sexual intimacy starts with yourself. I hinted at it a little earlier, but let's go deeper.

Cultivating your own desire

For many of us God girls, desire has been seen in a negative light. Desire has been portrayed as lustful, illicit, dirty, or shameful. What it has done is caused us to suppress desire. We don't want to be seen as "bad girls." From the time that we were little girls, the good girls were approved of. The bad girls were punished. Those were the girls who experienced discipline, timeouts, and sitting in the corner. Being bad meant that we were going to be isolated, alone, and rejected.

You may not think this has anything to do with anything, but it really does. Desire is beautiful and holy. While I do believe there is a time and season for everything, having desire before the season of marriage doesn't make the desire itself wrong. It means that you are normal. It is also normal to go through seasons of not feeling desire too. Now this is from the book of Karin. I will always tell you when it is. I believe that sex is something that you should never have to say "No" to. Let me clarify that.

As I said, I grew up with a lot of shame around the area of sexuality. I am a PK aka a Pastor's Kid. Like so many of us, I only received the perfunctory "just don't do it" talk. That was about it. No strategies. No deep explanations. Just, "God said don't do it." Because of all of my feelings of being rejected as a child, bullied, my not feeling beautiful, and the early violation of my sexuality, it created the perfect storm for me in my young adulthood.

I longed to be wanted and to be validated by a man's love or attention. I had so much guilt and shame about what had happened to me and a heavy dose of the fear of God about sex outside of marriage that I wouldn't be the girl who slept around with everyone. I did want to have someone to desire me and to see me as important and worthy. This emptiness in my soul led me to be in these ridiculously long-term relationships. In my mind, I was justifying my sexual activity because "at least we were in love." I told myself that I was always going to marry them.

Now to this whole idea of not having to say "No." I was riding the fence. Instead of having a bold clear stance that I was going to wait until I was married, I tiptoed and danced on the line and dipped back and forth across the line. After I had decided that I was no longer going to have intercourse, I still pushed the line and had loose boundaries with sexual activity but said "No" to intercourse.

After so many years of tap dancing between playing around and saying "No," I went through a period of sanctified sexuality where I was living totally celibate. Because I was getting married, I thought I could automatically say "Yes" now. I had a license to drive. I should be open and ready to throw my legs up. That didn't happen automatically for me. I remained shackled to the shame of yesterday unknowingly. I still felt sullied from the times that I didn't say "No" before marriage. Instead of having a clear stance and then using that sexual energy in some other creative endeavors, I just stifled it. I buried my desire. I acted like it wasn't there and that it was wrong to have it.

I know that there may be many of you who have felt the same way. Desire became this dirty word and now you struggle with lighting your fire. To be honest, it made me wish that I never even heard any of the stories of, "You shouldn't." I felt like at least I wouldn't carry the badge of shame.

Your desire is God-given.

Let's clear this up. Your desire is God-given. It is your divine birthright. Also, your sexual energy is not just about sex. It is that part of you that creates, that brings forth life. Cultivating desire allows you to be innovative in all areas of your life. It is that zest and enthusiasm behind anything great that you accomplish. Think about it. Have you ever had a grand project or mission that you completed? Didn't it feel like you gave birth to something? It's the same energy that fuels desire in your life. When you know what you desire and you honor it, you can manifest great things for you and through you.

Sometimes it's difficult for us to allow our desire to be because we've been told that we want too much. We've been told that we can't have, shouldn't have, or don't deserve to have. We've been conditioned not to ask for what we desire. We've been made to believe that we are ungrateful for what we have if we desire more than we have. None of this is true.

These limiting beliefs can stifle you from actually wanting God's best for you, not just in the bedroom but in life? One of my favorite passages in Scripture is Jeremiah 29:11, which says for "I know the plans I have for you, declares the Lord, plans to prosper you and not to harm you, plans to give you hope and a future." He also says in Psalms 37:4, "Delight yourself in the Lord and He will give you the desires of your heart."

Here's what I know Queens, not only will God give you what you desire, He will implant godly desires in your heart. Your desire for love, connection, passion, ecstasy, and orgasms; also deep sexual intimacy is a godly desire placed in your heart by God Himself. Stop ignoring your desire. Give it voice. Allow it to come alive. You've been so conditioned to be numb and unfeeling. Feel what you feel. It's safe for you to do it. You should not want for less. If you are not feeling that, it's time to examine why.

Grab your Queen Wife Journal.

Are you letting culture, society, or even church folks' stigmas about women and desires hold you back?

Have you been hurt and disappointed by your husband's actions or inactions with regard to pleasing you sexually? Or has his lack of care and tenderness toward you diminished your desire?

Have you just been exhausted, overwhelmed, and too distracted to allow desire to develop?

Have voices from the past made you feel like a "bad girl" and kept your desire at bay?

Is there a physical cause of this lack of desire?

I'm not sure why your desire is waning, but you need to investigate that. If you're able to rule out a physical problem, you've got to go within and determine what's affecting your desire. If there's a disconnect related to how your husband is treating you, it's time to talk about it. We'll tell you how in Part 3.

"Teach A Wife" Tip

What do you want?

Do you know what you want? I have a notebook that is entitled my "Book of Desires." In it, I write things that I desire in my life, inside and outside of the bedroom. I write in it frequently. I take time to go back and read it too. I give myself space and a place to pour out my heart and look at what I really want. That's the first step. You've got to know this. What do you want?

You came to the planet knowing exactly what you wanted. Babies know what they want and they are relentless about getting it. They express their needs and their wants. They will cry and cry until you give it to them. Whether it is hunger, a need to be changed, or just a desire to be held and rocked, they will let you know. As new parents, we begin to differentiate one cry from another. So what happened to these confident, self-assured beings? Little by little, we were talked out of our desires. We were told, "No." We were told, "You can't." We were told what to think. We were told what to feel. We were told what to want. Pretty soon, we became robots, carbon copies of those authority figures in our lives and the culture around us. It's time to break out of that mold.

Everything that's good ain't God for you.

You will never be able to get to a new destination in your marriage or in your life until you first know what YOU want. Not what "they" said that you should want. Not what your momma and them told you to want. Not what society said is popular. Not what the old ladies at your church said that you should have. They all might be good and godly, but is it what God said to you? Everything that's good ain't God for you. Once you realize what it is that you desire, then you can start taking steps towards getting it. The "How" or methodology to achieve what you desire will begin to appear to you. That's just the kind of God we serve. God will show you what to do. He will direct you to books. He will show you people to connect with. He will lead you to websites and seminars. Most of all, He'll speak directly to your heart. He will show you what you need to do in order to receive your desire. More importantly, He will reveal who you need to become to receive your desire.

Grab your Queen Wife Journal.

Take some time, quiet time, to reflect and to write the answers to the above questions down in your Queen Wife Journal. They will help you. Afterward, spend some time talking to your husband about your desires. In most cases, he will be thrilled to hear about your desires and anxious to fulfill those that he can do. If getting clear about your desire still seems difficult, consider working with a mentor to help you. You can connect with me at support@queensforchrist.org for a free Queen Wife consultation.

Plunge into pleasure

To improve your half of the sexual intimacy equation with your King, you must be willing to plunge into your pleasures. You've gotten clear on at least some of your desires. You've gone into your heart and mind and searched them out. Now, let's get into your body. To allow your sensuality to grow and expand, it's necessary to release any overthinking and allow yourself to experience the deep, visceral feelings of your body.

When it comes to pleasure, we've heard that self-care is not selfish. And of course you know you can't serve from an empty cup. Somehow, many of us don't believe it. We have denied our own pleasures so long that it's become normal. We are fully invested in pleasing everyone else and so poorly invested in pleasing ourselves. Please ourselves? That sounds selfish. We tell ourselves to just have a servant's heart when many times we're really being a martyr. Do something that pleases me? Heavens no!

I'm going to say Heavens yes. Queen, you need more pleasure in your life. This is not optional. We all do, and you shouldn't feel guilty for seeking it out. What gives you pleasure? What makes you feel good in your heart and mind? What makes your body feel amazing? What lights you up? Commit to giving yourself pleasure and receiving pleasure every single day.

"Teach A Wife" Tips

Hold me baby

We all need touch. Whether you consider yourself touchy-feely or not, touch is essential to your overall health and your pleasure. Did you know that if an infant does not receive physical affection in touch, it could actually die? It has been said that we as humans need eight hugs a day just for maintenance. Eight! We need touch. I'm convinced that little boys horseplay and jostle around in an attempt to satisfy their need for touch. It is completely socially acceptable for little girls to want to hug and hold hands with other little girls and to drape themselves over mommy or daddy. Unfortunately, early on we start to detach from giving our sons the same type of physical affection. They need it just as much as little girls do. Touch is principal for your pleasure and well-being. Your entire body is full of nerve endings that desire the pleasure of touch.

Pleasurable touch is powerful because it releases oxytocin. Oxytocin is the "cuddle or love hormone." It reduces cortisol, the stress hormone, and it allows us to bond with others. If you only receive touch when you are making love, you're limiting your pleasure. How can you increase the amount of touch you receive on a daily basis? Incorporate the eight hugs a day practice. Put your arm around kids. Place your hand on your friend's shoulder. Get a massage. Ask your man to give you one or give yourself a massage. Your body will thank you, and you will feel better on the inside. It's your self-love and self-care regime Queen.

Touch also helps to fill your pleasure cup. That is your responsibility. Your man should add to your desire and complement the pleasure that you are already holding within yourself. Take your time when you're in the shower to slowly, gently wash your entire body. Use luxurious soaps that feel great against your skin. Lavish your body with natural oils or quality lotions. Enjoy the experience of smoothing them onto your body.

Hold hands with your King. Cuddle. Snuggle up with your kids. My girls are teenagers now, but every now and then I'll take one of them on my lap and rocking-hold them like I did when they were little girls. I hug and kiss them every day. Get or give yourself a scalp and neck massage, or even a vaginal massage. Now we're talking. There are plenty of benefits to sensual massage. Take the time to fill your pleasure bowl with touch.

Pleasure scan

Where can you increase the amount of pleasure in your life through touch? Do this exercise. Your body is very wise. Sit down in a quiet place and fully relax. Take very deep belly breaths in through your nose and out through your mouth. Allow a smile to lift the corners of your mouth each time you exhale.

Put your left hand on your heart and your right hand on your belly. Scan your entire body starting at the top of your head. Ask yourself, "Where does my head need more pleasure from touch? What kind of touch does it need? How should it be delivered?" Go to your neck and then your shoulders. Work your way down to your feet. Write down whatever comes up for you.

Now, you can work on them. Give your body pleasure. When you're able to do this, it allows you to receive pleasure from your King and to give it to him in an elevated way. As the saying goes, put your oxygen (pleasure) mask on first.

I really got to use my imagination

I'm full of songs today. Now that you've worked on fulfilling your own desires and awakening to more pleasure in your life, it's time to use your imagination. You're already using it. Are you using it when it comes to your sexuality and your sexual intimacy with your King?

Sexual fantasy has gotten such a bad rap in the faith community. As I said before, your brain or your mind is your biggest sexual organ. If you are not using it to enhance your sexuality and enrich your intimacy, you're probably not experiencing as much pleasure as you could. One of the ways that I stoke the fire and desire for my husband is through my imagination.

I know we have a rendezvous scheduled for tonight or that I'm going to prompt one and I'm imagining exactly what I'm going to do to him and what he's going to do to me. It's like faith. You've got to see it before it comes. I like to see it before we both come. Your imagination allows you to be creative and to try new things before you try them. If you have any hang-ups about fantasizing, it might be time that you work on dropping that, especially if you want to have a more explosive and ecstatic sexual intimacy with your King.

Own up

Own up Queen. Own your desires and talk about them. Give yourself permission to experience your deepest heart's desires. Plunge into pleasure. Find what excites you and delights you. Ask for what you want. Open your mouth! A closed mouth doesn't get fed. Don't assume that he knows it. Don't put pressure on your King to figure it out. Tell him in a loving, kind way. Be true to yourself. Say Yes to life. Say No to things that you really want to say No to. Be okay with it. Be clear about the vision that you have for your life and for your marriage. Be the change that you wish to see in your relationship. If you want more passion, be more passionate. Be more passionate about yourself. Be more passionate about your man. Be more passionate about your shared vision. Be more passionate about love, life, and making love. Know that it is God's desire for you to have and enjoy your life with yourself and with your man. Make a decision that you will not settle for anything less.

Grab your Queen Wife Journal.

Go to the sections that stood out the most for you. What did you learn about yourself? What hadn't you thought of before? Where do you need to grow? Take your Queen Wife Journal and map out your next steps.

What a "Ho" Can Teach A Wife

CHAPTER 3

Naked and Unashamed

"The LORD God formed the man from the dust of the ground and breathed into his nostrils the breath of life.... Then the Lord God made a woman from the rib he had taken out of the man, and he brought her to the man..... The man and his wife were both naked and they felt no shame."

Genesis 2:7, 22, 25

What does it mean to be naked and unashamed? When God made mankind, he formed us out of the dust of the ground. He breathed into our nostrils the breath of life and man became a living soul. We know from the biblical account in Genesis that God saved the best for last. He created us in His very image and likeness and then gave us dominion and authority to rule and reign in the Earth. He released us to be fruitful and multiply. When God finished with His creation, He looked at it and said that it was very good.

In Genesis 2:22, God makes woman. He puts Adam to sleep and takes out one of his ribs. He takes the rib out because we were meant to be side by side. I believe He also chose the rib to form her because it is closest to and protects her man's heart. Catch that. Queen, you are the one who covers and protects your husband's heart. Part of your intimacy is that he allows you into his heart and you become a shelter for him to be able to share the deepest parts of himself. That's intimacy. He lets you see into his heart when he gives it to you. Are you a safe place for your husband's heart or do you degrade, demean him, and tell him to stop being "in his feelings"?

The passage goes on to say in verse 25 that the man and his wife were both naked and unashamed. We live in a society that is accustomed to covering up. We try to cover up our feelings and hide our emotions. We try to look unbothered and unconcerned as if that is a sign of strength and a badge of honor. Being able to be naked as a person and yet unashamed bridges between the sexual, spiritual, and emotional intimacy.

We are conditioned to hiding who we are. It's not safe to share our true feelings. We're looked upon as weak for having or displaying emotion, especially if you are a man. Being naked, allowing yourself to be bare, is seen as dangerous. Even in today's society where people willingly show most of their bodies in public and on daytime television shows with images that would have been considered soft porn when I was growing up, nakedness is seen as shameful. Mind you, there are things that require a level of modesty and decorum, in my opinion, but the human body itself is not shameful. It is glorious.

Naked and unashamed is a picture of not just our physical, sexual intimacy but of spiritual and emotional intimacy too. It speaks of a closeness that only you and your King share. No one should be closer to you than he is. If anyone knows the secrets of your hearts, it is each other. You are fully loved and accepted regardless of your faults or failures. You don't have to hide anything from each other because of that. You honor and protect each other. You can strip bare before each other in every way. There is no fear of judgment and condemnation in your Beloved's eyes or heart. It is the picture of total love and approval. That is how God is with us, and it is the process for how we can have the intimate marriages that God created us for.

Let's talk about shame

Shame is the feeling that something is inherently wrong with you. It is beyond guilt. Guilt is an awareness that you have done something that is wrong. It is related to an action. Shame doesn't have to do with an action. It is the consciousness of being seen by others in a negative light. Shame says that you are unworthy because of who you are. It's interesting how the garden story took a turn when Adam and Eve felt like something was missing from them. The feeling of shame started before they bit the forbidden fruit.

Whenever we see ourselves as less than who God says we are, we are dancing with shame and, as a result, will make poor decisions and try to hide or cover ourselves up. Your marriage is a relationship in which you should be able to be free. Let's consider body shaming for just a moment. I don't care how large or small you are, there will be someone who doesn't like it. Who cares?! You were sent here to be your best you, to be who God made you to be. God gave you an amazing vehicle, a sacred temple called your body. Don't let anyone shame you about your size, how tall or short you are, your hair, the size of your breasts, the way your teeth look, how wide or how slim your hips are, how round or how flat your buttocks are, or anything else.

Can I tell you that when you are with your husband, you are beautiful in his eyes? Be beautiful in your own eyes. It's difficult to be sexually free when you don't love your own body. Your man does not care about your stretch marks. He couldn't give a hoot about your cellulite. He's not bothered by your love handles. He just doesn't care. I realize that there are exceptions to this, but for the most part, our men don't care! They only care about you, wanting to connect with you, and being able to please you sexually and otherwise.

"Teach A Wife" Tips

The Queen in the mirror

I want to share something that has changed my whole life and invite you to try it too. Mirror work. I learned it from Louise Hay many years ago. Mirror work is one of the most powerful ways for you to honor and love on yourself. This one exercise will require you to be naked. I do this every day. Stand naked in front of the mirror and love on yourself.

Tell yourself that you are beautiful. Thank your eyes for seeing so clearly all these years. Thank your teeth and tongue for helping you to eat and enjoy wonderful tastes your entire life. Thank your heart for beating and your blood vessels for carrying blood throughout your entire body without you ever having to remind it to. Thank your skin for covering you, protecting you, and allowing you to feel beautiful sensations—hot and cold, soft and sharp. Thank your breasts for their beauty and how they may have nurtured and fed your children as well as provided you (and your King) with so much pleasure. Thank your womb space for housing your reproductive and sexual organs and being so integral to your sexual satisfaction. You get the idea?

How can you be one sexually or otherwise if you aren't thrilled about yourself? Be grateful for yourself. Appreciate all that your body's done for you. Tell your body what you want it to do. If you want it to be more sensitive and receiving of pleasure, ask it to. If Jesus talked to the fig tree and it heard and obeyed him (See Mark 11:12-21), why can't you talk to your body and it obey you too?

After you do your mirror work, write down how you feel. Was it easy to do? If not, why do you think it was difficult? What thoughts came up as you were in front of the mirror? Was your mind trying to distract you? Did you feel a little better about yourself? What did you notice about yourself that you hadn't noticed before? What are some things that you would like to say to yourself? How do you want to see yourself?

The "Nudie Booty Challenge"

Here's another tip. Spend a lot more time naked. That's right. Hang out in your birthday suit, even if it's just in your bedroom. Be naked and enjoy it. If you're not okay with it yet, do it in small doses until you feel okay with it. Can you start with just being bottomless or topless? Make the confession, "I am naked and unashamed." How would you feel if that were true? How would you carry yourself if that were a reality? Got it? Use your faith muscle and act as if. Who said that "36-24-36" was the only winning hand? Brick houses come in all forms and measurements.

Now you realize that I do mean being naked with your husband too right? Let's not be naked and just enjoying yourself and then when you see him coming, you throw a robe on because you don't want him to get any ideas. Queen, you need to be having some ideas yourself because you've cultivated your desire and plunged into pleasure. You're relaxed. You've filled your own cup. It's time to pour out. It's time to get it poppin. Men are very visually stimulated. They get excited with your clothes on, so imagine what will spring when he watches the curve of your beautiful behind sashaying by every night when you're in your bedroom together.

Can I tell you the truth? Your Beloved loves you and all of the curves of your body. A real man wants you and desires that you would want him too. He's exhilarated when you can just be confident in your own skin. When you can be uninhibited and fully present in the moment to receive pleasure from him, that's the ultimate turn-on. He's not worrying about your body's

71

"imperfections." There's no one who can make him feel as good as you do. Trust that.

Now, let me give this a little balance. This is not to say that you should just let yourself go and not take care of yourself. We all get older and many of us have gained weight over the years and parts of us have gone south. Length of years doesn't give you a pass on bringing your sexy back. You should want to take care of yourself and honor your temple for yourself first. It is the temple of the Holy Spirit. Treat it like God lives there because He does.

Eat nourishing food. Drink lots of water. Exercise. Move in ways that you find enjoyable. Keep it cute. Dress up. Get your hair and your nails done. Put on some make-up from time to time. Keep it hot. Let your outer adornment reflect the level of beauty that you are and of the woman that your man married: his Queen. I have found that when I take greater care of myself, I feel sexier, even if it didn't mean much of a big deal to Brian.

How has this Nudie Booty Challenge been for you? Did it allow you to feel more comfortable with your body? Did it stir up a little more fire and desire between you and your King? What ways would you like to modify it?

Grab your Queen Wife Journal.

Go back over all of the tips given in this chapter. What new thing did you learn? What are you willing to try right now? Where do you need to grow in your mindset? Write your thoughts in your Queen Wife Journal. What's next?

CHAPTER 4

Ready to Talk about the "Ho"?

I know you've been reading and reading and wondering, "When is this Queen going to talk about the "Ho"? I thought this was about what a "Ho" could teach me."

Well, we're about to dive in right now. I had to lay a little bit of groundwork first. I hope you can see the importance of first developing intimacy with yourself by understanding and acknowledging your own desires and creating opportunities to shower yourself with pleasure. In the words of Mother Maya Angelou, "You teach people how to treat you." How you do that is in how you treat yourself. If you want to be loved, adored, and cherished, start giving it to yourself first.

Again, everything in Scripture is to give us an example to live by, whether it is something we should do or something we should avoid. Most of us have heard about the Proverbs 31 Woman/Wife and have hailed her as our standard. She's not the only woman in Proverbs that we can all learn from as Queen Wives. Several years ago as I was reading the Scripture and meditating on this passage, I saw the wisdom in it and what we as wise women could learn from how the "Ho" carried herself and why men found her irresistible. King Solomon is giving a word of warning to young men. Let's examine the text in Proverbs 7:5-23. It reads...

5 That they may keep you from the immoral (strange) woman,

From the seductress who flatters with her words.

6 For at the window of my house I looked through my lattice,

7 And saw among the simple, I perceived among the youths, a young man devoid of understanding,

8 Passing along the street near her corner; and he took the path to her house

9 In the twilight, in the evening, in the black and dark night.

10 And there a woman met him, with the attire of a harlot, and a crafty heart.

11 She was loud and rebellious, her feet would not stay at home.

12 At times she was outside, at times in the open square, lurking at every corner.

13 So she caught him and kissed him; with an impudent face she said to him:

14 "I have peace offerings with me; Today I have paid my vows.

15 So I came out to meet you, diligently to seek your face, and I have found you.

16 I have spread my bed with tapestry, colored coverings of Egyptian linen.

17 I have perfumed my bed with myrrh, aloes, and cinnamon.

18 Come, let us take our fill of love until morning; let us delight ourselves with love.

19 For my husband is not at home; he has gone on a long journey;

20 He has taken a bag of money with him, and will come home on the appointed day."

21 With her enticing speech she caused him to yield, with her flattering lips she seduced him.

22 Immediately he went after her, as an ox goes to the slaughter, or as a fool to the correction of the] stocks,

23 Till an arrow struck his liver. As a bird hastens to the snare, he did not know it would cost his life.

This right here is chocked full of wisdom. Let's take it line by line with what this "Ho" can teach us wives. Hopefully, you're doing a lot of these things already, but can you take it to another level? Let's see.

1. Be strange.

Let's start right here with verse 5. In the KVJ, the "immoral woman" is called strange. It's sometimes meant a woman who was a foreigner, from a strange country. Here, it meant that she was a harlot, a prostitute, or what we call today a "Ho." What does it mean to be strange? It means unusual, extraordinary, or curious; it means odd; queer, or even surprising.

Are you strange? I'm not saying that you need to turn into some weirdo, but let's be honest Queens, sometimes we can become really predictable, usual, ordinary, and boring. This is not to say that he doesn't do the same thing. However, this is not about him. This is about you gaining some nuggets from this woman. You can only change you.

How can you remain interesting? How can you keep an air of

mystery about you? How can you keep yourself and your relationship fresh and alive? Check out these tips.

"Teach A Wife" Tips

a. Keep some separate interests.

While it's great to do a lot of things together, make sure that you have some separate interests as well. The old saying, "Absence makes the heart grow fonder," is true. There will inevitably be things that you enjoy that your spouse doesn't. That's okay. It actually allows for great conversation. You get to learn about things that interest him and vice versa. Keep doing things that allow you each to grow separately and together.

b. Maintain a sense of awe and wonder about your man.

It's very easy to fall into the "Oh it's just him again" feeling. You see him day in and day out, at his best and at his worst. Remember how wonderful he seemed when you first met him and you were just curious about getting to know him? Go back there. He is not the same man who you met or who you married. How can you allow a sense of awe about who he is to return to your heart or to increase it? Every day, recognize what's awesome about him and tell him.

c. Be spontaneous.

Change things up. Keep him guessing. He shouldn't always know exactly what you're going to do. It could be something as little as you sleep on the other side of the bed. Spontaneity can be exciting. Think about how you can incorporate more of it in your life with your King.

In closing, be strange Queen. The strange woman is alluring because she's fascinating and intriguing. So were you when you first got together, but life happens and we become unconscious and begin to go through the motions. Help him to realize that there is so much more to you. Leave room for excitement. Surprise him. Forget the schedule sometimes. Do things out of the ordinary. Keep the mystery. Keep the passion. Unleash that free-spirited woman in you. Keep him guessing sometimes!

2. Seduce that Brother!

Verse 5 also calls this woman a seductress. Let's stop right here. When was the last time that you seduced your man? I'm not talking about leading him astray like this passage is saying, but seducing him to make love to you. Remember, you've got a license to drive. Your marriage license. For many couples, the husband is often the initiator when it comes to sex. It also usually really turns your man on to have you come on to him too. I remember sitting in a marriage fellowship hearing a husband say that. He was sharing how men want to know that their wives find them attractive and desire them. They want to hear it. This was the second time that I'd heard this gentleman saying that. I wondered if his wife knew that he sounded very vulnerable and exposed. The seductress seduces him with her words. She knows what to say. She flatters him. Sometimes we think that flattery is negative, insincere praise. To the contrary, flattery can also mean to try to please by complimentary remarks or attention. There's nothing wrong with pleasing your man with loving and kind words. We will go deeper into this later.

Are you seductive? Do you even act like you want him? Does he come home and find you walking around the house in lingerie or, better yet, in the buff? Hey!! Do you send him the text to let him know it's your night and that you can hardly wait for him to get home? Do you kiss him goodbye in the morning and let them know what you are going to do to him later? Can you leave him the sexy note in his briefcase?

A seductress knows how to use her eyes to communicate desire too. She knows how to couple those alluring glances with mysterious smiles. She's out of her head and into her body and allows her body language to express her desire. Get creative in your seduction of your man. He's your man. It's honorable. God made it to be good and for both of you to enjoy it and initiate it.

3. Welcome him home with joy.

This might seem like a little thing. I promise you that it is not. After your man has been fighting the dragons all day, he wants a soft, safe, welcoming place to come home to. Do you stop everything and go greet him? Or, do you keep on doing whatever you're doing and just yell, "Hey!" or say nothing at all? Verses 9-10 says that in the twilight, in the evening, in the black and dark night when he was heading towards her house, she went out to meet him.

You might be busy getting the kids settled and making dinner, but just pause to acknowledge his presence and show him that you're glad to see him. The "Ho" does that. She makes him feel like he is the most important thing on her mind. I remember when I would hear the garage door open, signaling when my husband was arriving home, and I would roll my eyes. Honestly, I was not glad to see him coming. There came a point when I decided I was going to do all I could do to make our marriage work. I had to faith it. I had to think of how I wanted to be treated when I come home and the family is already there. I had to give him what I wanted even if I didn't feel it at first. Your feelings will follow your actions and your faith. Treat that man like a King and the King will come forth for you too.

4. Dress it up Queen!

Well, I know you've heard this before. Don't look better for the man at work than you do for your man at home. Verse 10 says there was a woman who met him with the attire of a harlot. In other words, she was looking the part. Do you look like your husband's wife? Your appearance is not just a reflection of you. It is a reflection of your husband and how he cares for you too. You better look good for your man. Most of all, look good for yourself and let him be the beneficiary of it.

Men are visually stimulated and motivated. Put on a cute dress or skirt. Show a little leg. Make sure your hair looks nice. You might not have on a full beat in terms of your makeup, but you shouldn't look ashy either. OK? Not all the time! You might be thinking, "But he doesn't put it all together for me." We aren't talking about him. Again, you can only change you. Be the example.

For nine years, I homeschooled my children. That meant I was almost always at home. I didn't have a need, in my mind, to dress up or to look a certain way at home. Something happened that changed all of that for me. I was at the Science Center with my girls taking them to a class. Afterward, we stayed in the play area and I looked around at the other homeschool moms that were there. I was shocked. So many of them simply looked as if they had no pride in their appearance and had not given how they looked a second thought. And this was out in public. From that day on, I've vowed that I would not look like I fit into the group that I saw that day. If they are happy with how they look, good deal. I knew for myself that that was not my standard.

Don't take your man for granted thinking that you already have him and he needs to just love you how you are. Although that is true, is that excellent!? Should you neglect yourself just because he put a ring on it? Get real with yourself about your appearance and find the balance that works for you. By all means, keep it classy. You deserve that, and so does your man.

5.   Hide it in your heart.

Verse 10 also says that this woman is of a crafty heart. The Hebrew word for crafty actually means "to guard" or "to keep secret." In other words, she is keeping secret things in her heart probably about her motives. This made me think of how Psalms 119:11 says that we are to hide God's Word in our hearts. What do you have hidden in your heart about your husband? Are you storing up love in your heart? Is there deep affection in your heart? Are you thinking about how you admire him? Check out this tip.

"Teach A Wife" Tips

A lil' appreciation goes a loooonnnggg way baby

Try this. Get out your Queen Wife Journal, search your heart, and write down at least 31 things that you appreciate about your husband. They can be large or small. For me, I appreciate that my husband is a man of God. I appreciate that he prays earnestly for our family. I appreciate his dedication to our covenant of marriage. I appreciate his deep love for me and for our children. I appreciate how he loves and cares for my parents just like they are his own. I love that he makes up the bed every day, etc.

Make your list. Each day I want you to meditate on one of those things. If it's the 13th of the month, look at number 13. Keep that on your heart for the entire day. Verbally affirm him and tell him that you appreciate him and why. Telling him why is very important.

Instead of hiding anger, resentment, and disappointment in your heart, opt for hiding love, respect, and appreciation for your man in your heart. It will make a huge difference in how you interact with him and how he receives from you.

6. Be loud and wild.

Verse 11 says that this woman is loud and rebellious. Now at first glance, this may seem out of place. It's not. Men don't mind you being loud, they just don't want you to be loud all the time. I take that back. There's one place that they probably do want you to be loud all the time. But, I digress. I will relate this to being confident and wild at heart.

What makes you wildly attractive is confidence. When you are confident in who you are and what you have to offer, it draws your King to you. Unless he's weak and insecure, every King wants a confident Queen.

Be wild at heart. Be free. Be free to be yourself authentically. I remember when I was in my little Christian Stepford Wife mode. While there's nothing wrong with a little give-and-take and serving, I was giving myself totally away for so long in marriage that I wasn't being myself. Although I was very competent and in some ways confident, I was not confident in my relationship with my husband. Pretty soon, I realized that this did not work. I was a raging volcano inside feeling like I could blow at any moment. I wasn't expressing myself. I wasn't allowing myself to be seen.

Pain is often a great teacher. The pain I experienced from not being true to myself finally freed me. I couldn't hide or deny my truth any longer. I had to stand in it. I began to do my own work. I worked with a mentor and coach. I had long talks with just God and me. I searched my heart and got to the truth of who I really was and what I really wanted, and I began to open my mouth.

I remember the day when my husband paid me the most beautiful compliment. We were in the kitchen talking to the girls and he said, "Your mom is much more expressive now." He didn't realize how much that meant to me that he noticed I was no longer Karin, the church mouse but I was Karin, the proud lioness. The funny thing was I was not that way with anybody else in life. It took a very long time for me to break free. I began to ask for what I wanted in a way that he could receive it. It feels so good to be able to confidently express myself passionately. I hope you have that same joy too.

As for the rebellious part of the "Ho," sometimes we need to rebel. We need to rebel against the false teachings that are keeping women stuck and small. We need to rebel against the notion that we are to be passive, second-class citizens in our marriages. That is not God's intention. You would be surprised, but there are still many people who propagate these untruths in the church even today. Marriage is the union of two equal partners. Rebel against anything that tells you contrary.

7. Be adventurous.

Verse 10 also says that this seductress will not stay at home. Now Queens, this is not to say that you cannot have plenty of adventures in your house. Let your imagination go wild there. But, leave the house sometimes. Spice it up. Go out and enjoy yourselves together. Check out these tips.

"Teach A Wife" Tips

Regular date night

I will interject something that has been a staple for our marriage. Every week for over a decade, unless one of us is out of town, my husband and I go out on date night. Sure we could watch a movie at home, but we leave the house and do something together. Especially when you have young children, it is essential that you take time regularly for just the two of you to connect and to have fun together. This is not the time to talk about the finances, problems at work, or struggles with the kids. Go out, enjoy yourselves, and do something entertaining with each other.

The value of vacays

I remember earlier in my marriage that a dear friend told me her vacation schedule for the year. One week vacation with the family. One week vacation with her girlfriends. One week vacation with just her King. Vacation is a core value from me, so I was totally down with that! Now, we haven't always been able to do that. Even if it is just for a few days, get away with your Beloved and do something different away from home. It does wonders for rekindling the romance.

There's something magical about being away in a beautiful hotel, resort, or B&B that turns my Clark Kent into Superman. Yesss! He can leave the stresses of life and the business behind him and totally put his attention on us. It's a great feeling. Trust me. Brian doesn't really like to do a whole lot of things. He is pretty simple. However, when I take him away from home, he often goes out of his comfort zone to try something new. He usually ends up having fun and really appreciating it. Get out of the house. Go to an arcade. Hit a bike trail. Visit your town like you are a tourist. Explore nature together. Whatever is an adventure for you, do it. Get out of the house.

8. Initiate, initiate, initiate!

Verses 12 said that this "Ho" was outside, at times in the open square, lurking at every corner. Sister Girl was on the prowl. She was waiting for a Brother. She had plans for him. Verse 13 said that she caught him and kissed him. She wasn't shy. She didn't hold back. She was assertive. Some would say that she was aggressive. However you interpret it, she wasn't waiting to be picked; she was picking her man for the evening out.

Now you have a man. A man that God gave you. A man that loves you. A man that chose you over every other woman in the world, Are you going after that Brother? I know he's already yours, but again, everyone wants to feel wanted. He wants to sense your passion and desire for him. If you've been more laid back, shock him and initiate your next tryst. Do a "no panties" week or two or month. Your love nest will thank you. Lean over or up against him so that he notices and give him that look. This works best with a skirt or dress for easy access. You'll have him coming home early and leaving home late. I promise you that your husband loves it when you take the lead.

9. All I want is you. Let's eat!

Verses 14 and 15 is where this seductress puts in work, Honey. What she is saying essentially is, "Listen Baby, I paid my peace offerings. I'm not out here in these streets for personal gain. Your girl is all fine. All I want is you. I want you in my house simply to enjoy the pleasure of you." She is letting him know that she has an abundance at home, and no one to share it with. She lets him know that she came out diligently looking for him. She's glad that she found him and can't wait to be with him.

Talk about talk. This behavior was so uncommon for women of the time. Her bold and brazen demeanor was probably coupled with the fact that she loved sex. Do you? Are you willing to tell your man how much you want him and put it into delicious words that cause him to anticipate the fulfillment of your seduction. If this feels uncomfortable, practice it. Write it down and say it into the mirror. Text it. Send him a voice recording. Make sure that you tell him to listen to it alone (lol). Not only is your man visually stimulated, most men love words of affirmation. I almost feel like it is every man's love language. Tell him. You want him. Tell him. This cannot be overemphasized.

On another note, you have heard that the way to a man's heart is through his stomach, right? I'll go deeper on that later. For now, this "Ho" is a woman of great substance and plenty of provision for entertaining this man. The peace offerings were offered to the priests voluntarily as a thanks for some mercy. These offerings were from the best flesh of the animals. Parts of the offerings were kept by the priest and the rest were returned to the person who made the offering. This food had to be consumed that day and was used to feast upon with friends. So there you have it. Not only was she offering him a night of great lovemaking with no strings attached, but she was also going to cook for him too? That's almost a no-brainer for him. Delicious food and satisfying sex fills two of your husband's greatest needs. Remember that.

10. Set the atmosphere.

Check Sister Girl out. She has set the stage for mind-blowing sex. Verses 16 and 17 say, "I have spread my bed with tapestry, colored coverings of Egyptian linen. I have perfumed my bed with myrrh, aloes, and cinnamon." She has set the atmosphere. She laid out her bed with the best linens and tapestry so that it looks inviting and delightful. The sheets, pillows, and bolsters are soft and comfortable to lay on. It's luxurious. She put effort into it. She has perfumed her bed. Not only does it look appealing, but it smells wonderful too.

This may or may not matter as much to your husband. Most of our husbands are able to focus so keenly that they could make love to us while the house is falling down around us. Maybe you think he doesn't care about what your bedroom looks like. You might think if he cared so much, why doesn't he pick his socks up off the floor. Can I tell you that your man does care, and he appreciates it when you lead the charge in making your house a beautiful home? Here's the bottom line. We're more likely to be distracted by the atmosphere of our bedrooms than they are. It's just how our brains are wired. Because of that, your setting the atmosphere and making your bedroom a love nest benefits your focus and feelings of passion, which also greatly benefits him. Clean that room up and make it a lover's den.

Another tip. You can take it or leave it. Try to keep your bedroom as the place for two things: sleeping and making love. Get rid of that blasted TV. You probably already have one in the family room. Leave those books in your office. This is not a classroom. Well in some ways it is, but you know what I mean.

If you can, even leave your devices in your office or another room too. Phones and tablets can be such distractions. You could be talking and connecting if it weren't for all those pesky notifications about nothing taking your attention away from each other. Think of all the time that you spend watching TV or online that could be spent together. Start small. Set the atmosphere for intimacy by removing distractions from it.

11. Give him your time.

Here's something that the "Ho" says to this young man. She's telling him, "I got time Baby and it's all for you." In Verses 18-20, she tells him, "Let's do it all night long. I'm here for you." She lets him know that he can have all of her as long as he can hang. Take your fill of this good stuff here. And just in case he's wondering, she assures him that her husband has taken a big bag of money and Daddy's going to be gone for a while. What can you get from this? All I have is time, and it's all for you. You are the only thing that's on my mind.

What can we learn from the "Ho" here? Several years ago, I remember sitting with a dear friend sharing about all the things that I was doing and about to do. She stopped me and asked, "Where does Brian fit into this?" I said, "He doesn't," and honestly, I didn't really care that he didn't. Brother Man was getting on my nerves at the time, real talk. She pulled me back to the fact that men need to know where they fit into our lives. So true.

Let's unpack this. Often times, we are the ones with the many, many roles. We are ourselves. We are wives. We are mothers. We are daughters. We are sisters. We are grandmothers. We are aunts. We are business owners or employees or supervisors. We lead church organizations. We are a part of civic organizations. We are soccer moms and football moms and lacrosse moms. We are friends. We are confidants. We are coaches and mentors. We are shoulders to lean on. We are. We are. We are and our lists go on and on.

Although, we say we are wives first, we are often not wives first. In our long to-do lists, being a wife gets pushed further from the top. We often feel like other people need us more. We sometimes get more fulfillment and appreciation from other people too. Real talk.

Although your King may have many roles too, he is probably not functioning in most of them at the same time like you are.

Where does he fit in?

Queens, we can get so busy trying to actualize and be all we can be. We can allow ourselves to be pulled in so many directions with the children's activities and our own that we just squeeze our husbands out of the equation intentionally and unintentionally. Many times, he won't say a word. He'll just find something else to occupy him. He might not ask for more time directly. You'll see it in the sadness in his eyes. You'll recognize it as he sits in front of the television. You might sense it in his irritation about you going to do yet another thing away from home and away from him. If you get still enough, you'll sense it in the loneliness in his heart and probably in yours too. Can you hear the cry of your unfulfilled hearts?

We can get so occupied filling our time with activity that is not taking us where we want to go. Do you want a hot, holy, happy marriage? If you do, you must put in the time. Yes, you need time to work on yourself, but you need more time to connect with your man. You need time to talk. You need time to sort things out together. You need time just to sit in each other's presence. You need time to make love. You need time to parent together. You need time to really open your hearts more or again. You must give him your time.

I had to learn this lesson and I'm still learning it. Believe it or not, I'm sort of introverted. I enjoy my own company immensely. Give me a great book and a journal, and I am great for weeks all by myself. Yikes! I grew up as an only child because my sister is much younger than I am. I can honestly deal with other people in very small doses. I have to be very intentional and give Brian time. I don't do it perfectly, but I'm always striving to be better at it.

12. Make him run after you.

How can I cause this Brother to run after me? Here's what the "Ho" is a master at. Verses 21 and 22: "With her enticing speech, she caused him to yield, with her flattering lips she seduced him. Immediately he went after her…" Before I started writing this book, my husband said this, "Babe, if you want to know what the 'Ho' does better than most women is she knows HOW to talk to a man. Make sure that you put that in your book." So, taken from a King on his throne. It's all in how. We will talk about this more later too.

For now, is your speech enticing? Do your words create an exciting hope or desire? That's enticement. Does he feel lavished by your words? Do your words pull him closer to you or do they push him away?

As you can see, there is much that we can learn from the "Ho." She has shown us how to talk to the King. She's shown us how to make ourselves irresistible to him. She's demonstrated to us how to set the atmosphere for physical intimacy and how to express our desire to him in a way that has him running after you.

Grab your Queen Wife Journal.

Take the wisdom that the Word offered in this chapter. Go point by point with your Queen Wife Journal and put a strategy together. What did your learn? What did you see in a new way? Where do you need to grow? How can you up-level? Put your thoughts down. Pray about them. Let God lead you.

CHAPTER 5

Gimmies the Benies

How are you doing Queen Wife? I hope you have gotten some very helpful information and inspiration to keep your marriage bed hot. Let's go a little further into why you need to have more sex than you're having. Besides all of the wonderful benefits that your sexual union provide for you spiritually, mentally, and emotionally, I want to share some physical benefits of how having sex regularly can improve your overall health. There are many, but I will just share a few to get you really focused on just how magnificent God designed your physical oneness to be.

Sex boosts your immunity

Physical intimacy strengthens your immune system. Researchers have found that people who have sex at least one or two times a week had higher levels of immunoglobulin A—an antibody that helps fight infections, viruses, and germs that lead to sickness. People who have more sex were also found to take fewer sick days. I'm not a doctor, but maybe you can skip the flu shot and just have a roll in the sack a couple times a week during the next flu season. Just saying.

Physical intimacy lowers blood pressure and reduces stress

Over 75 million adults in the US have high blood pressure. That is an astounding 1 in 3 adults. High blood pressure is often called the silent killer. It usually has no warning signs. It often has no symptoms, so people don't even know that they have it. It also puts people at a greater risk for heart disease, the number one cause of death in America.

Aren't you glad that God has giving us something satisfying to help in this area? When we make love, it releases "feel good" hormones into the body that help to ease stress and promote peace, pleasure, and self-assurance. They also prevent increases in blood pressure, especially during times of stress. In general, it works wonders for allowing you to release tension.

A roll in the hay improves your heart health

Studies have shown that when men have sex at least twice a week they are as much as 45% less likely to develop heart disease than those who do so once a month or less. Having sex gives the same benefits as exercising, which includes burning calories and strengthening your muscles. It also helps to regulate your hormone levels. Isn't that amazing? It's great for your heart—in your soul and in your body.

Getting some can lessen your pain

When we make love, it releases endorphins, which are our natural pain-relieving hormones. Sexual activity has been found to reduce headaches and migraines. Making love also can reduce or block back and leg pain as well as lessen pain from menstrual cramps and arthritis.

Making love gives you sweet sleep

We've all been there. You've just finished making love and before you can even settle into the crook of your husband's arm, he's fast asleep. After we make love, prolactin is released. It is the hormone that promotes relaxation. Additionally, oxytocin, which is released during orgasm, also boosts sleep and relaxation. I'm not particularly a napper, but the sense of peace and relaxation from an afterglow of making love can even cause me to tap out. Having trouble sleeping? Make love.

Doing it increases your sex drive

Have you ever thought that you did not want to have sex with your husband until you actually started doing it? Just do it. The more you have sex, the more you will want to have sex. Your desire for it actually increases. Also, the more frequently that you engage, it keeps your juices flowing by increasing your lubrication, your vaginal elasticity, and the blood flow to your sexual organs. In other words, the more you do it, the more you do it.

Knocking boots will make you look younger too. What?

You mean I can look younger by having sex? Yes! Now this is a benefit that we all can go for. Regular physical intimacy, as in four or more times a week, has been shown to not only help couples to look younger, but also to feel younger. Who knew that making love was also the Fountain of Youth?

These are just a few of the countless health benefits of making love. God knew what He was doing. Not only does it knit our hearts together and allow the two to become one, but it also provides increased health to our temples. Got it? Now go do it!

Grab your Queen Wife Journal.

What did you learn? Did any surprise you? What benefit do you want to see manifested in your life? Write about it and get to work!

CHAPTER 6

More that You Need to Know about the "Ho"

Okay Queens. Let's have a little more fun with this. I want to close this section out by sharing with you more that you need to know about the "Ho" and some additional thoughts on physical intimacy with rapid fire "Teach A Wife" Tips throughout. In my research for the book, I went to our Brothers and simply asked them, "Why is the 'Ho' so appealing to men?" I will share their responses throughout this section and other tips and tricks to get your sexual engine revving.

Let's establish one thing for sure. What you and your husband do in your bedroom is between you and God. As long as you are not incorporating other people into your marital bed, as the kids say, "You're Gucci." The Scriptures say in Hebrews 13:4 that we are to honor our marriages and to guard the sacredness of our sexual union. Let's face it, you have pledged yourself to each other until death do you part; that's a long time to be with just one person. Real talk. Since you are making this commitment, why not also pledge to do everything within your power to allow your sexual intimacy to grow, to flourish, and to be satisfying for you both. Promise to allow your intimacy to be renewed day by day, year after year.

These are some things that you may want to consider in keeping your union fresh. Marital oneness incorporates a number of facets of intimacy, which are interdependent of each other. I say that because you will see overlap between sexual intimacy and spiritual intimacy or emotional intimacy and even recreational intimacy. Look at each section and assess where you are. What is God saying to you about each area?

Are you ready?

Satisfying sex doesn't begin when you climb into bed with each other. It starts with what you did when you got out of the bed that morning. What you do at night is a combination of what you've done all throughout the day. If you have neglected each other all day and taken the other for granted, don't be surprised if you're not overflowing with feelings of love and passion when the lights go out that evening. This is exactly why your sex life gives an accurate temperature of your overall intimacy. Make sure that you fill each other's love tanks all throughout the day so full that your coming together is a natural outflow.

How do you spell love?

Now that is a good question. How do you spell love? Dr. Gary Chapman penned the book "The 5 Love Languages." In it, he details couples' emotional communication, or the five primary different ways that people feel loved, and how you can then interact with one another for greater intimacy and connection. I do recommend that you check out his work and look at his website to complete the free test to find out what your primary and secondary love languages are. Although quality time is one of those primary five love languages, I must say this again, I believe that quality time still spells a dimension of love for most people.

In order to make deposits into each other's emotional accounts, spending time together attentive to each other, still has to be a part of the equation. When can you dedicate uninterrupted time on a daily basis with each other? Brian and I often spend time very early in the morning together and then later in the evening, but our definite time is early. It's what works best for us. Before the sun rises and the kids are awake, we can come together to talk, share our day's activities, and just speak our hearts. When will that be for you?

Early morning snacks and smorgasbords

Although quickies can be quite satisfying, you may want to incorporate a variety of experiences in your sexual palette. Think of your natural diet. Sometimes a bagel on the run is cool. You don't have much time and you can wrap it up, take it with you, and eat it while you're driving. It's like a breakfast snack. Other times, you want a full, down home, country breakfast. That could include freshly squeezed orange juice and a cool glass of milk, fluffy banana nut pancakes topped with real whipped cream, Wisconsin cheddar scrambled eggs with spicy salsa, savory pork sausage patties, and pan-fried breakfast potatoes with onions and peppers. If you're serving that up, call your Girl. Morning sex can be wonderfully exciting, especially if you both have gotten a good night's sleep and are fully rested. Here's a tip. Your husband's testosterone levels are at their highest early in the morning, which is why many mornings he might even wake up standing at attention. O Happy Day! It's a great way to start the day and to put a big smile on both of your faces. Take advantage of your mornings; whether it's a quick hit or a whole spread, feast on that loving.

You better cook Girl

Speaking of food, I mentioned earlier about the saying, "The way to a man's heart is through his stomach." I know that in today's society, this may be a little off-putting. We want to be so liberated and in some ways a little androgynous that we don't want to attribute anything to the masculine or the feminine. Sure, you may have a man who cooks instead of you, but that's not the case for most relationships. Always find what works for you, but by and large, men are looking to you for domestic support. It is one of their greatest needs.

Part of that domestic support has to do with food. Providing meals is often a way of expressing love, and it is also often received as love too. Growing up and even today, my mom has always cooked. There was always something to eat at our home. We had family mealtimes. She waited on my Dad. Family not eating meals together or standing around eating is foreign to me. I have continued in that tradition. Some might call it old-fashioned, but you know what, it works. I don't cook every day, but I do cook most weeknights or have food available at home. I believe that there is something wonderful about sitting around the table eating and sharing.

When I asked men where we as women are missing it with them, they brought up this aspect of mealtimes. They said that if a man knows that when he gets home there's going to be a hot meal waiting for him and no drama, he'll gladly come home. I realize that every woman may not cook, but that doesn't mean that you can't have meals available. If you have to buy food and heat it up or just put it on your china, do it. If he cooks, then maybe you can at least serve it and clean up the kitchen. I believe that most men want to come home to relax and enjoy a delicious meal with their families. If I were you, I'd learn how to cook something. There are so many tools, free online tutorials, and simple recipes that can help even the most unskilled cook to be able to make something tasty. Even if you don't cook them yourself, at least have meals ready. Just my thoughts.

Be a sanctuary

When I asked the Brothers why the "Ho" was so attractive to them, one of the responses was that she is a sanctuary. If you recall, this was vividly portrayed in the last chapter about how she made her home a sanctuary. The house was clean. It was beautifully arrayed. There was food on the table. She was positive and all about him. Who wouldn't want to come home to that? While I agree that there are exceptions to every rule and there are foolish men who simply have inner struggles going on within themselves that preclude them from valuing how much their wives make their homes a sanctuary, for the most part, this is a part of that domestic support need that men want and appreciate.

Dr. Willard Farley talks about the domestic bliss man's fantasy in his book, "His Needs, Her Needs." He states that a man's fantasy goes like this. I'll paraphrase. The home life is stress- and worry-free. His wife greets him lovingly at the door with well-behaved children that are also glad to see him. His home is well-maintained. His wife urges him to relax before dinner, which he smells waiting for him in the kitchen. Dinner conversation is enjoyable and free of conflict. They enjoy an evening stroll, and the kids go to bed without a fuss. He and his wife can relax and talk and then go to bed and make love. Sound far-fetched? I don't think so. If I were a man, I would want that.

Their fantasy of a home that is a sanctuary of love, peace, and rest may seem one-sided. You might feel like I did for so many years. Why do I have to do all of this stuff? What is he going to do? It may look like we have all the responsibilities for working outside of the home and working inside of the home. I remember that wearying season of trying to do it all. I'll talk about that in Part 3. Here's the bottom line, if you need help in managing your household, you need to ask for it. Ask your husband to pitch in, get your kids to step up with their contribution, maybe even hire someone to come in from time to time. The truth still remains, he is looking for you to provide domestic support and a peaceful atmosphere for your home. This is big. It affects all areas of your intimacy. Take note.

What you don't want turned up

"Better to dwell in a corner of a housetop, than in a house shared with a contentious woman."

Proverbs 21:9

One of the other things that men told me about the "Ho" is that she knows how to turn down the negativity. She knows that he is coming to her many times to escape the constant conflict, nagging, or negativity that he may be experiencing at home. Nagging is a huge turn-off and a sexual intimacy blocker. Proverbs makes it very clear. A man would rather live in a corner than in a beautiful mansion with a nagging, arguing woman. Of course, this is not always the case, some men may like drama. Mostly, it is true. This is a continuation of the sanctuary theme. You might be thinking that it's easy for the "Ho" not to be negative with this man because she's not with him dealing with all his crap all of the time. You're right. The only problem is that you can be happy or you can be right, and sometimes you can be both.

It may be right that she's not there to deal with his annoying habits 24/7. She might not have to see all of his weaknesses on a daily basis. The truth still remains. If you are more negative in your relationship with your King than you are positive, there's a problem. If your focus is continually on what he is not and what he is not doing, you are headed for trouble. Even who you might consider the sorriest man alive has some good in him. One woman's trash is another woman's treasure. Remember that.

As women we have the amazing power to multiply. We are nurturers by nature. That can work for us or against us, depending on what we are choosing to nurture. If you are nurturing anger, it will turn into resentment and rage. If you are nurturing gratitude, it will lead to deeper love, appreciation, and connection. What are you going to focus on?

Additionally, we underestimate the power of our own influence. I have heard women say that if the man is the head, then the woman is certainly the neck. The power in being the neck is it can turn the head whichever way it wants to. While that may not always be true, we do have tremendous influence in the lives of our men. A man who loves you does care about what you think and feel. When we focus on the things that we desire for them and from them and lovingly express our gratitude for them and to them, we can see their response to our love with his changed behavior. Hang tight. Part 3 goes into this a whole lot more. For now, focus on being positive and affirming. Trust me. It's a game changer.

Grab your Queen Wife Journal.

Ask yourself these questions. Be honest.

- Am I pleasant, positive, and speaking life to my husband and about him?

- Do I exercise patience, or do I have a short fuse?

- How grateful am I?

- Do I express my gratitude to my husband and family?

- How well am I managing our household?

- Is our home relatively clean and well-maintained?

- Is my husband well-fed or does he always have to come up with something to eat on the fly?

- Do I give my husband a moment to decompress when he comes home at night?

- Do I pounce on him with all of my problems as soon as he walks into the door?

- Do I listen when he speaks?

- Do I respect him?

- If I were married to myself, would I be happy?

Fun, fun, fun

One of the things that the Brothers told me is that the "Ho" is fun. She knows that she only has him for a limited time, and the truth is she really often only wants him for a limited time. She gives meaning to the chorus "Girls Just Want to Have Fun." The crazy thing about this is you were probably so much fun when you guys first met. You were so easy-going. Your heart was open. You were willing to do things or try things just because they interested him. You would do what was fun for him even if it wasn't that fun for you just because you loved him and wanted to be with him.

It's called recreational intimacy. You might be surprised to hear this, but it is ranked as the second-most important need of men. You can even see the importance of it in how we relate to one another in ministry. Women's Ministries can get together and just talk, share, and be completely satisfied with that. That's not what men do. They gather around some type of recreational activity if they want there to be high participation. They'll go shoot hoops. They will play flag football. They'll hit the diamond and play baseball. They'll play golf or watch a game together. That's how they connect: around recreation. When we first meet our guys, we are often really open to that, being his hanging partner, but then might lose interest after marriage or after a while.

Dr. Farley states that most men really treasure the time that they get to spend recreationally. He says that recreation is something that our men plan for, look forward to, and will often spend considerable amounts of money to do things that they enjoy. If this need is that important, and it is, Wives you're going to have to discover what mutual recreational interests you can engage in. Google Dr. Farley's recreational enjoyment inventory. Fill it out. It has dozens and dozens of activities that you could engage in. Identify the areas that have the highest rankings for both of you and start having fun together again. It will build greater intimacy in your marriage.

Sex is NOT a weapon

"The marriage bed must be a place of mutuality—the husband seeking to satisfy his wife, the wife seeking to satisfy her husband. Marriage is not a place to 'stand up for your rights.' Marriage is a decision to serve the other, whether in bed or out. Abstaining from sex is permissible for a period of time if you both agree to it, and if it's for the purposes of prayer and fasting—but only for such times. Then come back together again."

1 Corinthians 7:4-5

This scripture is very clear here and tells us that the marriage bed, our sexual intimacy, is to be a place of mutual satisfaction. Your King is seeking to satisfy you, and you are seeking to satisfy him. It is not a place to use as a punishment or a reward. Sex is not a weapon to be welded against one another because you are angry. It is not to be withheld to punish your husband for not finishing a home project. Although your disappointment or some other marital strain can affect whether you feel close to him and want to make love to him, deal with that issue separately.

The Word is so clear. It tells us that we are to serve each other. Part of our covenant of love is that we will love each other unconditionally. When we marry, we are saying that we will do our best to satisfy the needs of our husband and vice versa. That may include making love when you don't really feel like it. While I don't think this should be the case all the time, there were plenty of times when I didn't feel like making love until things got going. Then I was really happy for that tap on the shoulder. That's normal.

Additionally, we need to have more sex than we're having in general. Everyone is different, but it probably would behoove you to make love more days than you're not. Sex is not a bargaining chip. It's not, "I will give you the booty if you will complete my 'honey do list' or, you didn't show up for me how I wanted you to, so no loving tonight." Poor communication is often the biggest problem coupled with a fair share of selfishness. We will go into that more in Part 3. Suffice it to say, do not use sex as a weapon. Sex is a mutually beneficial, integral part of a hot, holy, happy marriage.

You should only abstain from sexual intimacy for a short period of time that you both have agreed upon and if it's for the purposes of prayer and fasting. Notice that this scripture says only for that. Of course, there may be medical reasons why you need to take time apart, but then come back together. You do not want to put each other at risk in any way. Many times, our husbands feel loved because of making love. Do not neglect this very important means of communication and connecting with them at all costs.

Here's a little brief Sex Ed refresher

While we are both fearfully and wonderfully made, we are very different from our Kings in terms of our own sexual response. It is something that we both have to take into consideration to optimize our sexual satisfaction. Much of sexual fulfillment begins outside of the bedroom, but a great deal takes place in it. First let's explore the four phases of our sexual response and some tips for each.

Phase 1 is the excitement phase

For men, their sexual excitement is often visually created, develops very quickly, and does not require intense focus. Excitement in our Kings can come about in just a matter of seconds and he feels driven to move quickly towards orgasm. We, on the other hand, are quite the opposite. Our excitement is most often emotionally created and develops much more slowly. We have to consciously focus on our desires and pleasure, and if that focus is broken, it is much more difficult to regain it. If our Kings are like microwaves, we are like crockpots moving slowly toward orgasm. We require emotional connection, so romance is imperative to our becoming aroused.

In this phase, blood begins to flow to our genitals. The husband's penis will begin to stiffen and become erect. His testicles draw up closer to his body and his scrotum becomes thicker. Our labia, clitoris, and vagina will swell. Our vagina becomes more lubricated. It lengthens, our uterus rises, and our inner and outer labia spread apart to expose our vaginal opening. Our breathing and heart rates increase, and our muscles become tense. Our breasts can actually enlarge and our nipples become erect.

This phase can last minutes or hours. Again, sex doesn't start when you hop in the bed; it's something that can begin as soon as you wake up. Remember what we shared about desire and pleasure. How are you cultivating it for yourself so that you are ready when you do actually physically come together? Although this book is primarily for us, and to us this is where romantic connection becomes so important for us. Many times, our men just don't know what we find romantic. Why not share it with him?

> "...I want a man with a slow hand
> I want a lover with an easy touch
> I want somebody who will spend some time
> Not come and go in a heated rush

103

I want somebody who will understand
When it comes to love, I want a slow hand..."
Lyrics from "Slow Hand" by the Pointer Sisters

Focus on foreplay

The average man can be ready to rock and roll in a couple of minutes. Not so with us. We can take on average around 11-20 minutes or more to become fully aroused and ready for intercourse. Let me emphasize, fully aroused. Just because you're a little wet, that does not mean that you are fully aroused no more than the inside of your mouth being wet means that you're hungry. This is where our Kings could take the words from the Pointer Sisters' song to heart. They ain't never lied. Take your time. It will be much more pleasurable for you if you are totally aroused and ready to receive him.

Use your own creativity. Everyone is different, but here are a few ideas to get your creative juices and other juices flowing. Write a few of your own ideas too.

Grab your Queen Wife Journal.

- Send him a sexy text. You know what would turn him on. Yeah. Send that.

- Dance for your Beloved or with him. Nothing like a good slow grind to get the excitement going.

- Strip tease. Put on a sexy tune and one of his button-down dress shirts over your lingerie with high heels and let the show begin.

- Make a "Sexy" appointment. Go into his Google calendar or planner and put a "You and me tonight" appointment on it.

- Play a game of Strip (You Name It) Uno, Connect four, Tic-Tac-Toe, I don't know. Keep "losing" so that you can do the stripping. Winning!!

- Passionate kissing. OK, you know this, but how can you change it up? Ever kissed him from head to toe?

- Whisper sweet-somethings in his ear at dinner. The kids won't have any idea why Daddy's shoveling his food down so quickly.

- Pause your show or movie and lead him to the bedroom.

- Slide by him and give him a little booty as you pass by. He'll get the message.

- Take a sexy shower together. Take your time and lather him up really slowly. You might just get it on right there.

- Massage his scalp, shoulders, back, front. OK, you get the point.

Phase 2 is the plateau stage

During this phase, the sexual excitement continues to grow. It is the phase right before orgasm. Both you and your husband experience great surges in sexual pleasure. The muscles at the base of your husband's penis will begin to contract rhythmically. The clitoris can become extremely sensitive and start to withdraw under its hood to avoid direct stimulation. Your vagina becomes especially engorged and may turn darker. Prolonging this can lead to more intense orgasms.

The question of oral sex: Solly and Shuly

I started this chapter by saying that what you do in your bedroom is between you and God. Church folks always want to tell you what you can and can't do, especially about things that the Bible doesn't talk about. I do want to point out to you, however, that the Bible does talk about oral sex. Do your own research, but if you look at the metaphors in the Song of Solomon, you might get your whole life back.

"As the apple tree among the trees of the wood, so is my beloved among the sons. I sat down under his shadow with great delight, and his fruit was sweet to my taste."

Song of Solomon 2:3

OK. This seems pretty obvious to me. Solomon's bride, the Shulamite is sitting in the shade of the tree enjoying its fruits. Solomon, her lover is identified with the tree. Shade, fruit, and the apple tree are all ancient erotic symbols. Fruit and apples are symbols of the male genitals, which implies that she is enjoying fellatio, oral stimulation of her Beloved's penis. Alright now.

"My beloved is mine, and I am his: he feasts among the lilies."

Song of Solomon 2:16

Feasting among the lilies is thought to refer to kissing the tender part of each other's bodies. Of course this text does not mention terms such as the clitoris, labia, or vagina, but it is thought that this is the reciprocation of his pleasure and enjoying cunnilingus, oral sex, on his Beloved bride. Work it Solomon.

And there's more all throughout the text. Don't take my word for

106

it. Do your own little research. You might be pleasantly surprised.

Tightening up the garden

OK. Since we're talking about oral sex, let's talk a little bit about taking care of your vagina for great sex. First, sometimes we can be sensitive about our scent. Although a healthy vagina's scent is pleasant, it is an area where we wonder if it is from time to time. I heard Dr. Oz explain it this way. He said your vagina is a self-cleaning oven. You really don't need to stick anything up there to clean it. We can get a little overzealous about how we're cleaning her and cause imbalances. Many doctors recommend just using water or a very mild, unscented soap when you wash her. Be gentle. No harsh scrubbing. Ditch the wipes, sprays, and for goodness' sakes the douches. Summer's Eve can be gone.

Trim your pubic hair rather than shaving it. Shaving can cause irritation. Opt for cotton undies since they are breathable. If at all possible, go without undies. Your vagina loves to breathe. Try to stay away from thongs. Most thongs are not made of breathable material and can provide a greater breeding ground for bacteria because the material lies directly against the skin between the vagina and anus. They also tend to rub against the delicate skin around your vulva and clitoris, causing tiny tears that create access for microbes. That is no bueno.

Exercise that Baby with kegels. Kegel exercise strengthens our pelvic floor muscles, which also helps to tone our vaginal muscles. This can heighten our arousal by giving us the ability to tighten around our husband's penis during intercourse, which leads to more intense orgasms.

Lube it up. Lubricators are your friend. Keep them bedside. You want intercourse to be as smooth as possible. Also, dry fingers touching your inner folds can be extremely irritating. A little lube on your fingertips, on his, on the head of his penis or your vaginal opening can make sex so much more satisfying. Avoid anything that is petroleum-based. By the way, organic coconut oil is a great natural lubricant and is something that you can massage onto your vagina every day just for overall comfort.

Watch what you eat. If you have ever breastfed, you know that what you eat will affect the taste of your breast milk. The same is true with your Secret Garden. Try to incorporate foods like green vegetables such as celery and parsley. Also try cinnamon, yogurt, raw honey, and an array of fresh fruits including pineapples and oranges, mangoes, watermelon, strawberries, blueberries, and cranberries. And of course, drink plenty of fresh water. That's good for everything.

Phase 3 is the orgasm period

The plateau stage often ends with the Big O. During orgasms, the engorgement in our genitals and muscle tension reach their peak and are then released through a series of quick rhythmic contractions. Contractions can take place in the lower pelvic muscles around the sexual organs and anus, or all over your body. Most of our husband's orgasms are accompanied by an ejaculation. On average, our husbands can reach orgasm in as little as two minutes. Of course, no man wants to admit to being a two-minute Brother, but I digress. The average woman takes about 12 minutes to reach orgasm. Of course, this can be longer for both. This is the reason why we need much more connection, foreplay, and romance to get us over the hump.

Us and orgasms

Miss C

As women, we are blessed to have the ability to have multiple, long-lasting orgasms and in a variety of ways. We most commonly hear about the clitoral orgasm and with good reason. The clitoris is often in the center of pleasure for many women. Although it appears small in size, the clitoris is actually close to four inches in length. It is made from the same erectile tissue as the head of your husband's penis. We often see just the head of the clitoris, which is under the clitoral hood, but there is a whole network of pleasure there. There is also the clitoral shaft, the urethral sponge, more erectile tissue, glands, vestibular bulbs, and the clitoral legs that run underneath the skin. Its only function is to create pleasure with over 8,000 nerve endings in it, which is twice the number of nerve endings in the glans of your husband's penis. Let's just say that we have an entire pleasure treasure map that when properly explored can lead to mind-blowing sexual satisfaction.

In 2017, a study published in The Journal of Sex and Marital Therapy found that about 37% of American women needed clitoral stimulation to experience orgasm. Another 36% of the women said that although they did not need to have clitoral stimulation to reach their orgasm, it certainly made it much better. What that says is that the majority of women need and/or enjoy clitoral stimulation in order to reach a climax. Interestingly enough, only 18 percent of the women indicated that vaginal penetration alone was enough to bring them to orgasm. For this reason, it does well to focus on your pleasure and foreplay. This is not selfish. This is to ensure that you both are fulfilled. It takes far less for our Kings to reach an orgasm, so for the most part, you might want to make "Ladies First" your focus.

The G-Spot

The G-spot is believed to be an extremely sensitive area inside the vagina, less than halfway up the front wall from the vaginal opening. It is also referred to as the urethral sponge. When the G-spot is stimulated, it is said to cause powerful vaginal orgasms. It can be found if you or your King insert two lubricated fingers into your vagina and motion your fingers as if you are saying "Come here." It is located about 2 or 3 inches from your vaginal opening on the top side of your vaginal canal and is much more easily locatable when you are aroused. There are a number of sexual positions that will allow you to hit this spot more easily, including cowgirl and doggy style. Both give you great access for clitoral stimulation as well. You can also reach it in the missionary position if you lift your legs up around your husband's shoulders to tilt your pelvis for deeper entry.

The A-Spot

The A-Spot is a sensitive crevice located on the belly side of the cervix. It sits between the front vaginal wall and the ridges of the cervix. The cervix blocks the area from stimulation, which makes the zone feel extra sensitive. Penetration or even light touching of the cervix is uncomfortable for many women, but touching the A-Spot or anterior fornix can produce an immediate feeling of pleasure for others. To reach this spot, try the Bow or the Slope positions. Both allow for the deep penetration to hit the spot. You can easily find diagrams of these online for more guidance.

Playing with toys and tools

Alright. I guess I have to talk about it. About a year ago, I was talking about this with one of my girlfriends. She said, "Why are church folks so uptight about sex? People in the world have a problem

with sex and they go ahead and get a toy or tool and keep it moving."
I understood exactly what she was saying. I will say this again. What
you do with your husband in the privacy of your bedroom is your
choice. For the record, I don't see anything wrong with using toys and
tools to enhance your sexual intimacy.

If you couldn't walk well, you wouldn't feel shame about getting
a cane or a walker. Well, maybe you would, but you shouldn't in my
opinion. If your husband is having issues with his erection, what
is wrong with using penile rings? Men can have an orgasm from
intercourse alone. Most women cannot. I don't see any problem with
using a toy to help with bringing more mutual satisfaction in the
bedroom. I'm just saying. As long as both of you feel comfortable
with it, go for it. You've been playing with toys since you were a child.
Who said that you had to stop just because you're an adult? Selah.
That's all I'll say on that. Cheerio!

Phase 4 is the resolution stage

During this phase, the body gradually returns to its unaroused
state. Our heart rate and blood pressure will decrease. Your husband's
penis will become flaccid. Often, he is predisposed to dropping
off to sleep very quickly because of the hormones released during
orgasm, including prolactin. We, on the other hand, are often still
very much alert and because of the heart connection and feeling of
greater intimacy, may want to talk. We are also able to, with further
stimulation, quickly reach multiple orgasms. Our Kings, however,
often need a recovery or refractory time before being able to become
fully aroused and reach orgasm again. That period of time could last
from several minutes to hours or even days before he can ejaculate
again. How long is often related to their age. Due to these differences,
we must be understanding of each other's physiology.

There are a variety of online resources and books that will help you in your journey to greater sexual satisfaction. I highly recommend my Queen Sister, Gail Crowder's book, "Keep Your Legs Open: A Wives' Guide to Sexual Satisfaction." It is a short read that is packed with great resources including an illustrated sexual position guide. Yes! I'm sure that you will enjoy it as much as we have.

And another thing...

"And He Himself gave some to be apostles, some prophets, some evangelists, and some pastors and teachers, for the equipping of the saints for the work of ministry, for the edifying of the body of Christ, till we all come to the unity of the faith and of the knowledge of the Son of God, to a perfect man, to the measure of the stature of the fullness of Christ..."

Ephesians 4:11-13

Sex & your marriage is a ministry Girl!

Sex and your marriage is a ministry Queen. Yes it is. If your husband is your first ministry, your sexual intimacy is one of your most powerful outreaches. Do you hear me? I want you to think of this in terms of the five-fold ministry gifts. Now I encourage you to open your heart and release some of your theology. Hear what I'm trying to say. Let's look at those gifts.

The Apostle is a foundational gift and is sent as an ambassador of God to establish His heart toward His people and to build the body of Christ. Will you allow God to use you as His ambassador of love towards your husband? Will you let your marriage's foundation be built on the love of God as it is expressed through your heart to him and deepening sexual intimacy with him?

The Prophet is also a foundational gift and brings forth revelation and spiritual direction to others. As you minister to your husband Queen, God will use you prophetically to speak life and to decree and declare what He is showing you about yourself, him, your marriage, and your family. Be bold and unafraid. Tell your husband what you see. Tell him how to please you in life and in the bedroom. Show him things that are to come.

The Evangelist gathers. She is anointed to go out and share the good news that draws others to God. Queen, you are anointed to draw your King to God and to yourself. As you see the God in him and share what is good about him to him, he will be drawn to you. Within you is the power to restore anything that has been lost in any area of intimacy in your marriage.

The Pastor is the shepherd and is married to the sheep. She is anointed to feed, to nurture, and to care for the body. You too have the ability to feed the King in your man. You have the capacity to nurture his greatness. There's no one who can take care of him like you can. As you minister to him in this way, your connection becomes stronger than ever in every way.

Lastly, the Teacher teaches. She illuminates God's words. She reveals truth and helps the people of God to mature. God will use you to shed light on what He has spoken about you both, to enable your marriage to mature and to manifest the passion, love, friendship, and joy you both desire. Be His vessel.

As you read all of this, it may seem a little overwhelming. May I encourage you that you are the woman for the job? When faced with the question of "Why do I have to be the one who does this? Why can't he do something?" Dr. Emerson Eggerichs puts it this way, "May the most mature one step up."

Why you? Why not you? In you is the power to create; to establish;

113

to tear down what is blocking the power, purpose and destiny of your marriage; and to build it up. Why not you? Please know that I am standing with you as a Queen on the path to my own greater version of my hot, holy, and happier marriage every day too. Let's go higher together!

Grab your Queen Wife Journal.

Wow! This chapter was full of information and inspiration, tips and tools, imagination and calls to action. Do you feel challenged to have more passion in your marriage? Are you creating a bigger vision for physical intimacy for the two of you?

What did your learn? Did anything surprise you? Where can you shift your thinking? Did anything that you read clear up a misunderstanding for you? Where can you arise?

Pour your heart out and discuss it with your King. Get ready for Part 2 as we discuss The Holy: Your Spiritual Connection. The final section of this chapter was actually added in later and is a great segway into the next part of our journey together. God always knows what He's doing. Onward and upward!

PART TWO: The Holy

Your Spiritual Connection

What a "Ho" Can Teach A Wife

CHAPTER 7

Spiritual Intimacy: The Three-Fold Cord

"Though one may be overpowered by another, two can withstand him. And a threefold cord is not quickly broken."

Ecclesiastes 4:12

Spiritual intimacy is the lifeblood of a marriage of faith. It is so much more than just reading the Word of God together. It is living your life knowing and acting like God is present in every part of it. Guess what, He is. When you really think about it, it is the foundation or the center from which all other intimacy should emanate.

Too often, we separate God from certain areas of our lives. God, you can tell me about the Bible, but leave my bedroom alone. I'll figure that out myself. That's not to say that you don't need to get some education. You do, but even in your sexual intimacy, issues and hang-ups are most often not just physical. There's usually something going on in your heart and/or mind that is affecting your sexual union. So, especially in the bedroom, while you learn, pray. Seek God. Hear His voice for you. Your marriage is unique and deserves customization from the Spirit of God.

What spiritual intimacy is

Let us add to our definition of intimacy. Intimacy is defined as feeling close to another. It is being understood, feeling validated and cared for, and having a close connection with another person.

Spiritual intimacy is the foundation upon which all other genuine intimacy can be built. It involves your personal intimacy with God and your marital intimacy with Him.

Here are some characteristics of spiritual Intimacy in your marriage.

1. A deep abiding commitment to God

Your commitment to God comes first. "In him we live and move and have our being" (Acts 17:28). Everything and everyone starts and ends with God. We are because He is, so above each other and anyone or anything, our commitment to God comes first. What does that mean? It means that we trust in God. We believe in Him. We give our whole lives to Him. When both of you come together from a place of a deep and abiding commitment to God, you can work through anything.

2. Your God purpose

There are so many things that we can do in life, but it doesn't mean that we should do them. God has a specific purpose for each and every one of our lives. Having a spiritually intimate marriage means that we are open to tapping into our individual and collective purposes in life and love together. We have to place God at the center of it all if we want it to work.

3. Communication and communion

All throughout Scripture we hear where God says to call upon Him and He will answer. The foundation of any relationship is communication. It is at the center of our spiritual intimacy with God and each other as well. It must be cultivated by communication. It grows when we share our hearts and pour them out before God and each other. It is fostered by the time, the communion that we spend with one another in His presence simply listening, and allowing Him to minister to us.

4. Assurance of God's love

Lastly, our spiritual intimacy with God is built on us knowing and feeling that we can lean on Him. When we know that God loves us and wants the best for us, we can feel safe. The Scripture talks about God as a shepherd. Shepherds will do everything and anything to take care of their sheep. They will fight off predators. They will lead and guide them into safety. They will make sure that their flock is attended to and cared for. That's the same love and attention that God has for us and our marriages. He is with us to help us and to knit our hearts together in love as we allow Him to.

Grab your Queen Wife Journal.

What is spiritual intimacy to you? How do you see it reflected in your marriage? What areas would you like to see a more mature and vibrant spiritual intimacy between you? Write what comes up for you and share it with your husband.

What a "Ho" Can Teach A Wife

CHAPTER 8

Stop the Hindrances to Your Spiritual Intimacy

In the last chapter, we talked about what your spiritual intimacy is. Let's explore what it is not. Sometimes we get hung up on things that are not essential. We allow things to block our spiritual union. Let's take a look at what some of those hindrances are to our spiritual intimacy so that we can release them and go forth in the oneness that God intended.

What spiritual intimacy is not

Spiritual intimacy is not about religion. It is not about having a list of rules and regulations to follow. Let me just take a little side note. Now this is from the "Book of Karin." You can take it or leave it, but I feel that I must say it. Jesus did not come to set up another religion. He really came to point us back to God. He came to show us our oneness with God as our Father. That's why the religious folks of His time had a problem with Jesus. "How dare you come here talking about you and the Father are One. You are just a man. Blasphemy!!" they contended.

Jesus came to show us what being in complete union with God was like and that it was what God desires with us. It was all about us having a deepening, intimate relationship with Daddy. I believe that Jesus is probably sitting on the throne shaking his head looking at all of the politics and foolishness that we as people have put into religion that He never intended. It's always been about our relationship with God, our oneness with Him, and about having a dynamic connection to the living God.

What is stopping your spiritual intimacy?

What gives? What is stopping our spiritual intimacy? Like in many other areas of marriage, we have often had few real role models with regard to building spiritual intimacy with one another. However, here's the truth about this and anything. When we seek, we find. Regardless of whether we saw it in our upbringing or not, whatever we really want with all of our hearts, we will go get it.

The old saying holds true. "If you really want something, you'll find a way. If you don't, you'll find an excuse." Now, don't get me wrong, I'm not implying that all of these are simply excuses. They may feel like valid reasons to you, but if you peel back the layers, ask yourself if they really are excuses for you. Are these merely the things that you're using so that you don't have to do the work or take a risk of being vulnerable and spiritually open? Think about it. What is holding you back as a couple from your spiritual intimacy or any other forms of intimacy?

Grab your Queen Wife Journal.

Before you read this section, write what comes up for you about the above questions.

Hindrances to our spiritual intimacy

1. Importance and priority

How important is it for you to create spiritual unity in your marriage? It is the foundation of a marriage of faith. Too often we allow busyness to get into the way of it. Busyness is a way of feeling accomplishment because you're in constant movement. However, busy does not always mean productive, and it can become an enemy that is a hindrance to all intimacy in your marriage.

Have you ever noticed that you feel closer when you are on vacation or on a short romantic getaway with your Beloved? Why is that? May I submit to you that it is because you have chosen to slow down and give attention to each other? In building spiritual intimacy, we must find a way in the process of living to make it of utmost importance and priority on a daily basis.

2. Inflexibility

I can speak to this completely. When Brian and I got married, one of the reasons why we were both attracted to each other was because of our love and passion for God. We both had strong relationships with God and were deeply committed to daily devotionals, prayer, worship, and study of the Word as individuals. Trying to make that work jointly was a struggle.

He had his way of doing it and I had my own. It was sort of like trying to mix oil and water. Both are great ingredients, but they tend to separate. Have you ever tried to make your own vinaigrette at home? All of the ingredients sort of separate in layers. In order to get them to come together, you have to shake it up. It always seemed like I was the spices, the ingredient on the bottom. It felt like it had to be his way or it wasn't going to work. Finally, we stopped trying and just did our own thing. We weren't willing to shake things up and to be flexible enough to allow ourselves to come together as one. This has become one of my mantras, "I am flexible and willing to change." You will have to be flexible to build spiritual unity and any intimacy.

3. Undercurrent of anger

Let's face it. Marriage is messy. He seemed like Prince Charming until you got him home and no longer are dealing with his "Agent" aka the wonderful image he has been projecting. Don't point at him. We do it too. We may have seemed to be like a Royal Princess that quickly turned into Cherry from the movie "I'm Gonna Git You Sucka." Remember how they go to her house and then decided to be "honest" with each other. She turned into another woman, peg leg and all. "Don't make me hop after you!" I know. I know. It's hilarious how we wear those masks when we are dating almost unconsciously. We can fear rejection so deeply that we will be or project who we think we need to be in order to attract and keep who we think our spouses desire.

When the stuff hits the fan and real life ensues, it can lead to a lot of anger and offense. We sometimes let things slide over and over again and molehills become mountains. Have you ever felt like that? You're just ticked off about life and a lot of it relates back to your husband. If you are feeling this way and haven't read John Bevere's book, "The Bait of Satan," stop, do not pass go and get a copy now. That undercurrent of anger will keep you from being able to bond with each other, and it will drive a huge wedge in your spiritual intimacy. It's difficult to be intimate with anyone who you feel a great deal of negative feelings towards. You will have to resolve them.

"Make every effort to live in peace with everyone (that includes your husband, Queen) and to be holy; without holiness no one will see the Lord. See to it that no one falls short of the grace of God and that no bitter root grows up to cause trouble and defile many."

Hebrews 12:14-15

Every morning, new mercies are available for you. God gives us favor just because He loves us. We must be committed to extending that same grace to our husbands.

4. Failure to forgive

Let's take this a step further. When your King does something to hurt or offend you and you refuse to forgive him, that will destroy your spiritual intimacy. Here's another bunny trail. I read a book by Edwene Gaines about prosperity. She believes that one of the biggest blocks to our prosperity is our holding on to debts against others. In the Lord's Prayer, we ask God to forgive our debts as we forgive our debtors. Are you carrying financial debts in your life because of the debts that you hold against others? That's killing your prosperity in life, financially and otherwise. Gaines states that there is one way to know if you have forgiveness work to do in your life. Do you have a body? If the answer is yes, you have forgiveness work to do. We all know that God commands us to forgive, but do we? Forgiveness is a mandatory ingredient in your vibrant relationship with both God and with your spouse. If you are conditional in your love toward your Beloved, this lack of forgiveness will block your spiritual oneness and all intimacy.

"Bearing with one another, and forgiving one another, if anyone has a complaint against another; even as Christ forgave you, so you also must do."

Colossians 3:13

5. No respect

Rodney Dangerfield was a comedian who built his whole career on sharing ways in which he got "No respect" from anyone in his life. He really was funny. Unfortunately, respect for a man especially is no laughing matter. We all want respect, but your King needs it. Ephesians 5:33 says, "So again I say , each man must love his wife as he loves himself, and the wife must respect her husband."

Paul was making a point of emphasis. He was letting us know something of grave importance. He wanted to reinforce that the man must love his wife. He is commanded to love us sacrificially the way that Christ loved the church and gave himself up for her. In addition, he says that we as wives must respect our husbands. Here's another love language for your King: respect. If you have not read Emerson Eggerichs's book, "Love and Respect," add it to your library and devour it too. Just as we desire to be loved unconditionally, our men desire to be respected unconditionally too. It is how they receive our love through respect. You don't have to be perfect in order for me to respect you. None of us is perfect in our expression. Again, this is where we as wise women can unconditionally love our husbands by showing them respect. Where there is no respect, there is little or no spiritual intimacy.

Grab your Queen Wife Journal.

Now that you have read this section, what do you believe have been hindrances to your spiritual intimacy? Do you see yourself in any of the reasons noted in this chapter? Are you willing to change and make adjustments so you can be more united spiritually? Will you forgive yourself and your husband? Take some time to hear what God is saying to you. This will take humility and vulnerability. Write what comes up for you, and when you are ready to, humbly share it with your husband.

What a "Ho" Can Teach A Wife

CHAPTER 9

Building Spiritual Intimacy

The God-shaped hole

I believe that inside each and every one of us is a God-shaped hole that only He can fill. We might try to fill it with fame or success, with money and materialism, or even with our husbands or children, but only God can fill that hole. I believe the same is true in our marriages. There is a longing and yearning within our marriages that can only be satisfied by our drawing nigh to God together.

"Draw nigh to God, and he will draw nigh to you..."
James 4:8

Our spiritual oneness is potent. The fruit of it builds and revitalizes all facets of our marriage and our lives. God says in Jeremiah 29:11 "'For I know the plans I have for you,' says the Lord. 'They are plans for good and not for disaster, to give you a future and a hope.'" Many times, the missing link in our marriages is how we link up with God together. God has a good plan for our marriages. His plans are for good. His plans are to prosper us. His plans do not include disaster. His plans for our marriages are full of hope and a great future together. We only have access to those plans when we come together and allow God to fill them out for us. There is nothing that will create more unity in your union than endeavoring to have a shared commitment for your lives with God. This sense of spiritual discovery is the longing of our hearts. Throughout this chapter, I will share numerous strategies or "Teach A Wife" Tips. Take notes.

1. Separate but equal?

We all know about the era in American history when the ideology of "separate but equal" ruled the land. The problem with that way of life is that for many African-Americans, the separation meant that we were not receiving equal access or equal resources as our white Brothers and Sisters. Change had to come. We are still sorting that out in the annals of history.

As couples, we can get into a place of our own spiritual growth where separately we are soaring but there's no growth in our spiritual intimacy together. We're separate and it doesn't equal joy with God together. I know many couples who simply give up trying like we did time and time again. They lean only on their relationship with God individually. This is akin to leaving money on the table. Have you ever been in a negotiation in which you made an offer and they accepted so easily? You knew that you probably left some money on the table, meaning that you could have gotten more out of the agreement.

God wants us to get more out of our agreement. Amos 3:3 states, "Can two walk together, unless they are agreed?" and in Deuteronomy 32:30 it tells us that one can chase a thousand and two can put ten thousand to flight. What we sometimes miss from this text in Deuteronomy is that our ability to multiply our power comes from our allowing God to be our rock as we go at life together. Read the text. God gives tremendous power when we two come together. Queens, we absolutely must have our own relationships with God. It starts there. We must also be open and willing to cultivate a relationship with God and our husbands together.

2. Your way is not the only way

Sometimes Queens will say that they feel unequally yoked. It seems this way because they have a mismatched spiritual life with their husbands. They might feel like it is difficult to connect with their spouses spiritually because they're not in the same place spiritually. While this may be true, it is certainly something that you needed to have examined prior to marriage. If you're already in it or you started out going the same direction and you have ended up on different pages, let's talk about it.

I want to be really frank with you my Sisters. Sometimes we just think that our way is the only way. We have been sold a bill of goods that women are just more spiritual and more spiritually mature. While that may be true for some and perhaps in your relationship, please understand that your way is not the only way.

Sometimes our Kings feel spiritually inadequate because of our spiritual arrogance. Yup. It's true. If this feels prickly to you, it's probably for you. If the shoe fits, put it on. By no means am I telling you to hide your shine or to tone down your fervor for God in any way, but you also don't need to flash it in an attempt to make him feel small, as if your showing him up is going to motivate him to go after God the way that you do. I know that some of you are mad right now.

Listen, he may not be as fluent in his prayer life as you are. He may not speak in tongues and turn around and give you an interpretation. He may not know all of the Greek and the Hebrew of the Old and New Testament words like the Bible scholar that you are. Can I be real with you? Sometimes we look at those things and we are impressed. We feel so erudite and scholarly, and many times we look like Pharisees and Sadducees.

Luke 18:9-14 illustrates this point. Jesus is talking. I just love Him

131

because Jesus was such a real Brother. He tells a parable about the tax collector and the Pharisee. Right up front, this scripture says that Jesus shared this for all of those self-righteous folks who wanted to judge and put down other people. So both men go to the temple to pray. The Pharisee starts out saying that he's so glad that he's not like "those people." He then rolls out of litany of charges against "those people" and then has the nerve to direct one of them at the tax collector who's in the temple praying too. This is how you pray to God? The Pharisee goes on to say how he is so wonderful because he fasts and tithes. Outward acts don't always match your inner heart. The tax collector stood a distance away and wouldn't even lift his head up. He merely said, "God please be merciful to me because I know I've sinned." Jesus said that the tax collector was the one who was justified because everyone who exalts himself will be humbled and everyone who humbles himself will be exalted. Who are you? Do you have the attitude of the Pharisee as if your stuff don't stink too? Are you in so much self-deception that you think you do no wrong? Or, do you have the heart of the tax collector who is humble, self-aware, and willing to change?

"It's not always where you are but where you came from."

Queen, I'm speaking to you as a Sister who knows this. Religion has a way of making people very mean-spirited and judgmental. I used to be that way. When you have a religious spirit, you forget all of your stuff just because you're doing "the works." It's so easy to move from a place of love to a place of self-righteousness where you are putting everybody down in the name of trying to be holy. Now of course you are supposed to live holy, but I would love for you to read your Bible and look at Jesus's life. Jesus had the most beef with the religious folks. Those were the people who worship God with their lips but their hearts were far from Him, and they sought to impose a whole lot of man-made rules on people. Check out Matthew 15:8-9. Those were the folks who felt like they were the only ones who had it all together. They did not have a heart of love, mercy, and compassion towards people. They were more concerned about the letter of the Law instead of the Spirit of the Law. I hope you can hear my heart on this.

Now, back to our Kings. Just because your man has a very simple, plain way that he is with God, it does not mean he is not as close to God as you are. Yeah I said it. Spiritual growth is not based on how many scriptures you can quote. I know people who can quote the Bible from Genesis to Revelation and are as mean as rattlesnakes. Our spiritual growth is based on our becoming more like Christ in our lives. Remember this. It's not always where you are but where you came from. Spiritual pride is kryptonite to your spiritual intimacy. If I'm talking to you, humble yourself Queen. If not, share it with your cousin. She might need it. Your way is not the only way. Where you are is where you are and where he is, is where he is. Give your husband space to grow in his way and allow God to work in his life. Pray for a Brother instead of judging him. Real talk. I'm just saying.

3. Talk about God

This may seem like a no-brainer, but your spiritual intimacy will grow stronger if you have heartfelt conversations about the things of God together. Let me emphasize: talk about it and not preach to or at each other. This is not a competition of who knows what and who has a deeper revelation on what. Just share. You really have nothing to prove or to defend. This is not the time to get into a debate. OK ministers?

Talk about what God is doing in your life. Let your King into your relationship with God. Share what God has been showing you in the Word of God about you. What do you believe God has been saying about your marriage? What has God shown you about how you can improve in your life? What video or teaching has given you spiritual inspiration?

Talk about those things together. Listen attentively to each other. This is not to say that you should not challenge something that is way off. For instance, if your husband comes and says something crazy like they all had multiple wives in the Old Testament so he thinks you two should bring somebody else into your marriage, "Nah Brother." Pull him up on that, but by and large, God has not called you to be Holy Ghost Jr. in his life or vice versa. Loving, supporting, and encouraging each other in the Word is key, but it is how we do it that matters most. We will talk a lot about communication in Part 3 of the book, so hold tight.

4. Pray together

We have all heard that half of marriages end in divorce. Do you know how you can reduce the possibility of divorce in your own marriage to only 0.001%? Here's how. It is through regularly praying together. David McLaughlin, in his teaching series "The Role of the Man in the Family," shared an astounding statistic. The divorce rate for couples that regularly pray together is about one in ten thousand. That is about .001%. That's amazing! So why aren't we hearing about this? Why does it work?

When we pray together, not only does it open our hearts, but it binds them together. There's something very unifying about seeking God together. When we are committed to pursuing God individually and jointly, we feel closer to each other and closer to Him. The operative word is commitment. We must be committed to putting in the spiritual work of praying together and allowing God to move in our lives. He's a gentleman. He won't just barge in uninvited, contrary to what some religious folk may say. The Spirit of God will not make you do anything. We are free moral agents, and we live based on choice.

The family who prays together stays together.

I spoke a little while earlier about being flexible. When you are first starting out, how you do it is really not as important as that you do it. Don't get hung up in the "have tos" or the "shoulds." Leave all of your theology in your individual war room. Just get started together. What's important is seeking God together, not the method of prayer. As you become more comfortable with praying together, you can branch out into methodology. Sometimes you may just need to sit in silence together and let God do the talking. You can share what God said to you. Prayer is a two-way communication. It's not just you speaking to God, it is also God speaking to you. God also hears the silent prayers of your heart. Again, what's most important is that you pray. Pray individually. Pray together. Share the concerns that you have. Be vulnerable. Allow your spouse to see your heart, and ask him to pray for you. Here are a few tips that can help.

a. There is beauty in simplicity

Just keep it simple starting out. You may start out just having a quick word of prayer around the dinner table together. Perhaps you pray with each other before you leave for work. That's what we do. Or you might start with having a prayer night once a week when you really go into deep prayer together and bring your prayer requests for each other and loved ones to pray about them. Just start. Even if it's just for a few minutes, share your heart with each other and go to God.

b. This is not a prayer competition

I touched on this already, but you are not trying to impress each other about how holy your prayers sound. Straight up, this is a conversation with God. You can leave the "thous" and "thuses" out and just talk. This always amuses me. If you don't talk in King James English on a regular basis, why do you feel like you have to use that when you're talking to God? Just a thought.

135

c. Be straight up

We're talking about building greater spiritual intimacy right? This is not the time to keep your prayers cute. Let go. Admit you're crazy and ask God to help you. This is when you want to reveal your secret faults so that you can clear them out and receive the love and support you need from God and from your husband. Don't hold back. Admit your faults and ask for help. James 5:16 says, "Confess your faults to one another, and pray for one another, that you may be healed. The effective, fervent prayer of a righteous man avails much." There is a release that takes place in confessing your faults to God and to your husband. There is power that is released into your situation as your husband prays for you. Believe that.

Trust me. Nothing is more intimate than that. I remember one early morning when Brian and I were talking. He was admitting something to me that was a "weakness" of his. It wasn't anything salacious, but it was something that could be seen as a character flaw. It was in that moment that I realized I was not being as open with him because I would have never shared that with him, and it really wasn't that big of a deal.

It made me aware of some of the masks that I had been wearing. I was unwilling to confess my faults with him and creating a barrier to our intimacy. Let me give this some balance. Sometimes, we don't confess our faults because our spouses use them as a weapon later or even in that moment. Instead of being a place of love and acceptance, it turns into judgment. It sounds like, "Yeah I knew something was wrong with you." I mean wrong with you as a person, not that you just are unsettled about something. Be careful about that Queen. Of course, this goes both ways, but be gentle and non-judgmental, or he may never open up again.

Since then, I have found that some of the most tender moments in our marriage have been when I have been willing to lift the veil and show him my pain or weakness. When I felt weak and expressed it, he stepped up and has been my strength. He has shown me his unwavering commitment and support. That is sometimes hard for us to do Queens. Real talk. We are so used to being strong (whatever your designation) women. In my case, a strong black woman. In my community, so many of our men have been absent physically, or there and still absent emotionally. That is something that we have to work through and allow ourselves to trust our Kings. Allow your husband to be a container for you, to hold space for you. He has a desire to protect you. Let him do it as you open up through prayer.

d. Be consistent

You must make praying together a consistent habit. Do it every day no matter what. A short prayer is better than no prayer at all. It's better to have a consistent time or occasion in which you do it. Even if you have missed that daily scheduled time, before you go to bed, pray together. Be committed and consistent to it.

Everything that you place on the altar is altered.

5. Worship together

Worship is an intimate act. It is when we love on God, adore Him, and show reverence towards Him. In true worship, we humble ourselves before God. We recognize and esteem Him. We pour out our hearts before Him. We allow ourselves to be bare in His presence. In worship, we are transformed by the power of His matchless, all-consuming love being showered back on us. As you and your King engage in authentic worship of God together, it changes you. Your hearts become more tender and united. This may take place as you worship together in your local fellowship. I find it to be even more

137

transformative when you can worship together in the sacredness of your own home. Schedule some times of worship together, just the two of you, and watch how your intimacy is renewed. Place your hearts together on the altar of worship.

6. Be careful about your expectations

While I'm certainly not trying to rain on your parade, be careful about your expectations. God can certainly move supernaturally when we are open to receiving; however, in most cases change is gradual and not instantaneous. You didn't get where you are in your life overnight. You probably will not turn the tides that quickly either. Always have an expectation of God doing something great in your marriage through prayer. Understand that the change in the marriage is precipitated by changing you.

Expect that you are going to have to change. Keep an open heart so that you can hear when God is prompting you to get into alignment with His will for your life and for your marriage. Instead of looking at your husband wondering why the prayers you have lifted about him haven't manifested, take a closer look at yourself. Ask God what needs to be pruned from your mind, mouth, and attitude and then follow suit.

1 Peter 3:7 gives a stern warning to our Kings. It says, "Husbands, likewise, dwell with them with understanding, giving honor to the wife, as to the weaker vessel, and as being heirs together of the grace of life, that your prayers may not be hindered." In other words, it is saying if our husbands do not dwell with us in an understanding way and honor us as if we were a weaker vessel that needed or rather deserved attentive loving care but with the knowledge that we are equal heirs to God's grace, their prayers would be hindered. (Side note: We are not weaker. God just says for them to treat us as if we are. We are more refined in ways. You don't treat a juice jar like you do fine crystal. You handle it differently.)

God is saying, "Look man, if you don't treat my baby girl right, your life won't work." Now this is from the Book of Karin, but if you don't treat him well, your life isn't going to go well either. Selah. Do your man right. Ask God how you can be more loving, honoring, and respectful toward your King. How can you serve him? How can you out-love and out-give him? Then, be like Nike and just do it.

7. Get into the Word together

Your spiritual intimacy can grow exponentially when you come together and study the scriptures. Perhaps you will allow a book that you are reading to guide that. It could be a devotional or just a book on a specific subject. Marriage books are always great. I'll talk about that in a moment. You could also take a theme from Scripture such as walking in love and search out verses together or even individually and then come together to share what God spoke to you about the theme.

Why is this important? As we study the Word of God, it allows us to learn about who He is. It also shows us who we are. When we incorporate our experience with God and openly share it with each other, it draws us closer together and to God. Your marriage has purpose. There's a reason why God brought you together. There are treasures deep within each of you that will enhance your lives together beautifully. Go deeply into the Word of God and bring those jewels forth.

8. Study the Word with other couples

I highly recommend that you spend time with other couples through a marriage ministry fellowship or Bible study. Although we as women are often open to sharing and oftentimes do so freely with each other, it's important to be around other couples so that you don't feel alone. It's easy to feel like you are the only one having a struggle, but when you are in the company of others and you're able to see that they struggled and overcame, it gives you hope. Iron sharpens iron.

This open, heartfelt sharing is normal for most women. It is not as normal for men. It would be wonderful for your spouse to be a part of a men's fellowship, especially one that is either focused on married men or has a lot of married men in it. At the very least, a marriage ministry fellowship can expose both of you to support that can allow you to draw closer to each other and to gain wisdom and understanding.

9. Attend a marriage retreat or conference

We say that our marriage is at the top of our list, but how much focused attention do we give to learning and growing in our marriages together with God. You are married every day. At least once a year it would behoove you and your marriage to get away and go to a marriage retreat or conference. Giving focused attention to each other, your marriage growth, and seeking God together is not optional if you want to strengthen spiritual intimacy. When you get away and do it together, it's like breaking up the fallow ground of your heart, fertilizing the soil, watering it, and putting in new seeds. They will grow. Make sure that when you come home you have a plan of action of how to go deeper into what you have learned and to continue in your growth together.

10. Study a book on marriage together

This is a wonderful way to share and to gain understanding about each other. You could even do it with this book or any other book on marriage. Read it aloud together and pause to share your thoughts on what you have read. Take note of where God is pulling on your heart. What is He saying to you both about your marriage based on the information that you read in the book? Search out the scriptures about the subject? It could spin off into another study together. Make it fun. My husband and I both love to read, so this is something that brings us joy. Find what works for you.

11. Serve together

Another way to build spiritual intimacy is to serve together. Perhaps you are part of a ministry at church together. It could be serving in your community together with a cause that is important to both of you. God calls us to serve one another. In fact, He says that the greatest is a servant. When you have a mission that matters to both of you and you are able to serve others in that mission, it draws you together spiritually. What mission do you both believe in? What are some ways that you can serve together to bring that mission to pass?

12. Dream big together

Another component of spiritual intimacy unfolds when you are able to dream together. It may start with you creating a space for each of you to openly and honestly share your own dreams and desires. Are your dreams safe in your husband's hands? What about his?

Honor those dreams and treat them with care. Look for ways to support one another in your individual dreams and seek ways to merge them or to create big dreams that you can share with each other. There's research out there that shows that many of our fights are related to contention on the level of our deepest dreams and desires that are not being respected or accepted.

You may not get his vision completely, but be open to understanding it. Be willing to heal the disappointments of the past that may be standing in the way of you trusting each other to dream together again. Too often, we spend too much time lamenting over something that's already happened instead of forging forward into the good plans that God has for us now and in the future. Your spiritual intimacy will grow when you dream together.

Dreams create hopes. They stir up excitement and expectancy. We will talk a little more about this later, but for now, begin to think about your dreams and write them down in your Queen Wife Journal. Ask God to speak to you about His plans and the hopes and dreams for your marriage together. Write them down and come together and share them.

Your marriage has a purpose, and deep down inside you long to create a shared pursuit through your marriage. Purpose creates a beautiful partnership between the two of you. Make God's purpose for your lives together and individually a priority in your life.

13. Be like Christ

When you read Ephesians 5, you will see that marriage is about much more than the two of you. Our marriages are the vehicles by which we are to reflect Christ in the world. God wants our unions to be a living, breathing reflection of Him. When we make our spiritual intimacy our aim, the love, joy, peace, and prosperity that follow testify of God's love in us, through us, and as us. As we selflessly love one another, through all of the ups and downs of marriage, we get to exemplify the love of God to everyone that we encounter. It's so much bigger than you and me. Your marriage, our marriages affect everyone. God is calling us higher. It's time that we let it make us more like Christ so that we can live the divine life God sent us here to live.

Some closing thoughts

If there's one word that I use more than any other, it is the word "together." Live life together. It's very easy to fall into parallel lives. When it was just the two of you, it might have been much easier to focus just on each other. As children are added to the mix and careers and businesses get busy, you can easily slip into two ships passing in the night. Trust me. I know this all too well.

As I shared with you, I was a single mother when Brian and I met. When we got married, Brian instantly became a husband and a father at the same time. Having a blended family has its own set of challenges. One of them is that you don't have that time alone from the beginning with just the two of you. OK. That didn't come as a surprise to God, and He has a way to cause all things to work together for our good when we seek Him.

Sometimes when we quote Jeremiah 29:11-14, we don't read it in its entirety. The scripture reads:

"For I know the thoughts that I think toward you, says the Lord, thoughts of peace and not of evil, to give you a future and a hope. Then you will call upon Me and go and pray to Me, and I will listen to you. And you will seek Me and find Me, when you search for Me with all your heart. I will be found by you, says the Lord, and I will bring you back from your captivity..."

God has a fantastic plan for our lives, but we have to call upon Him. We have to go to God. We have to pray to Him. It is incumbent upon us to listen to Him. We must seek Him until we find Him. We must search for Him with all of our hearts. Then God says that we will find Him and that He will bring us out of our captivity.

"Prayer changes people. People change things."

Seek God Queens. Seek God for your lives together. Pray. Earnestly pray with and for your husband. I know there's a popular adage that says, "Prayer changes things." It doesn't. Prayer changes people. People change things. Real talk. I've seen people who have prayed and prayed until their tongues were about to fall out of their mouths and nothing has changed. So is God a liar? No. If we want our lives to change, we have to change. If we want our marriages to change, we have to change.

Let your prayer be the starting point. Seek God so that you can find the will of God. Then, get ready to change because you will have to. The best part of this is that you can do it! Keep this in your mind and heart...

"I can do all things through Christ who strengthens me."
Philippians 4:13

You can build deep spiritual intimacy. You can have a life that is rich in God's love and purpose together. You can overcome every obstacle in your marriage through the love of God. You can have the hot, holy, and happy marriage that you desire and God intended.

Grab your Queen Wife Journal.

I'll be honest with you, this chapter alone can transform your whole marriage. As we have said, your spiritual intimacy is the foundation of it all. It is possible for you to take one principle per week and focus on building this spiritual muscle between you for an entire quarter.

Which strategy spoke to your heart the most? Did you feel any conviction about any of these ideas? What would be your top three that you feel the two of you could start on right away? Write whatever comes up for you. As always, use it to inspire conversation between you and your King.

What a "Ho" Can Teach A Wife

PART THREE: The Happy

Building a Happy Marriage

Welcome to Part 3 of the book. We've talked about the hotness and your physical intimacy. We just finished the holiness and your spiritual intimacy. Now we're going to go through a series of chapters about how to have a happier marriage. I don't know about you, but if I'm not going to be happy, then what's the point? Seriously? I do not believe that God wants you to be forever miserable in a relationship. If His endeavor is that we might have and enjoy life, that doesn't sound like being unhappy to me. While there may be seasons of discomfort, it should not be constant but instead be leading somewhere better. In the next chapters I will share with you what I found that has allowed me to live a happier, more joyful life with my husband. Enjoy it. More than that, change.

What a "Ho" Can Teach A Wife

CHAPTER 10

What's Love Got to Do with It?

We've all heard the song made famous by the iconic Tina Turner asking the question, "What's Love Got to Do with It?" Looking at her unfortunate, tumultuous, abusive marriage, it would be easy to understand why she might record that song. The interesting thing is this is not really a song that hails love. It's more of an anti-love song. It's saying, "Hey Dude. This is just physical. This has nothing to do with love. Love is not a part of this hook-up here." When I researched the song, Tina actually didn't connect with it. It wasn't what she believed about love. It was merely what her agent thought would sell. He was right.

What kind of love is this?

We touched on this a little earlier in the book. Love has everything to do with your happy marriage. To clarify, let's talk about the kinds of love that exist. Scripture talks about four different types of love. Greek and Hebrew, the languages that the Bible are written in, are much more vast and varied than English. In English, we say, "I love pizza" and "I love my husband." Same word but different meanings. Let's explore the loves that we see in the Bible.

First, there's "storge." This is what is described as familial love. It is the love that you would find between a parent and child. Second, there's "phileo." This typifies brotherly love or friendship love. It is the same root for the city named Philadelphia, whose motto is "The City of Brotherly Love." Next is a love that we have talked about. It is "eros." This is romantic or sexual love, like the love between a husband and wife or two lovers. And lastly, we find "agape" love. Agape is the God kind of love or the divine love that God provides. Agape love is the foundation upon which we must build our marriages. It is a love that is completely unconditional. There is no "I love you" if, when, or because of what you say or do. All of the other forms of love shift and can change. Agape love is constant. It is consistent. It is secure because it is based on the choice of the giver, not the receiver. Here's my big claim. Marriage is a vehicle by which two people can learn and grow into unconditional, agape love.

Agape love doesn't just come naturally for the carnal or egoic. You can't live this out of your flesh. The ego likes to keep score. It lives to make sure things are fair. That's not agape love.

Agape love is a choice. We make it based on God's love. It really doesn't have to do with your husband at all. God so loved that He gave. In response to His matchless love, because we are so loved by God, we give that same love to others. Now who do you think God ordained to be the biggest recipient of His love through you? Why your husband of course. I want you to get that in your mind and heart. This relationship is teaching me how to be who I really am. It is showing me how to live love. It is grooming me how to walk like the god that I am. Jesus did say "ye are gods." (John 10:34) Lowercase G. Marriage calls on every faculty within us to prove that right.

I love him, but I don't feel in love with him anymore

I know that there may be many of you Queens who have lost the fire and desire for your marriages because you just honestly aren't sure if you are "in love" with your Kings anymore. Let's talk about that. Here's the truth. Falling in love is very exciting. It's the time when we are getting to know each other and everything is new, fresh, and exciting. It is that time when we have all kinds of butterflies. It's when we don't want to get off the phone at night. Remember that? You will go back and forth saying, "You hang up." "No, you hang up." You couldn't get enough of each other. Remember when you used to fall asleep on the phone together?

I was still doing that in my late 20s when Brian and I were dating. What sometimes we don't realize is that "in love experience," which is really in some regards infatuation, is a neurological response. It is like a brain cocktail. We are literally drunk on love. However, you might be shocked to know that this high seems to dissipate within about 18 months for most people. I always say that love is blind, but marriage will open up both of your eyes. What you could ignore or didn't even see before because you were under the influence of the brain chemistry of love, now you see it clearly and straight on, every day.

Marriage causes a shift. After the dissipation of these hormones and neurotransmitters when your body is no longer flooded with all of these feel-good chemicals, you get to clearly make a choice to love. Falling out of the romantic stage is normal and natural and necessary. It makes way for a more mature, lasting love. Did you hear that? It is when the real work of love, true love, agape love begins.

God school is in session

Hear me Queen. God school is in session. It's called your marriage. Marriage allows two people with different ideas and different perspectives to be able to learn and grow together in unconditional love. I'm telling you that when I began to look at my marriage as the school for me to learn how to love like God does, it changed my perspective on how I looked at Brian and our relationship challenges.

Are you willing to do that? This perspective inspired me to love Brian no matter what. It helped me to see him how God sees him. It changed me.

Great expectations

You know it's very easy for us to feel loved when our partners are measuring up to our expectations. What about when they are not? What about when they have failed miserably? What do we do when we feel disappointed because they are not responding the way we expect them to? We've done X expecting Y and they give us Z? What then?

We are still talking about learning to love unconditionally. I promise you. This shift in thinking will allow you to be happy no matter what. One of the biggest stumbling blocks in our happiness in marriage is unmet expectations. I'm certainly not saying that you shouldn't have any expectations at all. That would be ludicrous, but sometimes our expectations are unrealistic and leading us to offense. I recommended this book earlier. If you have ever read John Bevere's book, "The Bait of Satan," then you know how offense is such a slippery slope.

When thinking about your expectations I want you to ask yourself a few questions. Are these expectations realistic? Am I asking my husband to do something that only God can do? Let me give you an example. Sometimes Queens are expecting their husbands to fill them up and to make them feel good about themselves. They are looking for all of their validation to come from their husbands and are dependent on their Kings to make them feel approved of. In my opinion, that's an expectation that will never be fulfilled, as these Queens are looking for their men to meet needs that can only be provided by God; it should be between them and God. No man can ever fill a hole that was designed for God.

Cake and icing

I like to put it this way. The work that I do to fill myself up, to establish my sense of self, to secure my own identity, and to validate who I am is done between me and God alone. Brian does not complete me. We complement each other. I was complete when he found me even with all of my baggage. A healthy marriage is between two complete individuals. One plus one equals one. So Queen, if you're looking for your man to complete you, you're barking up the wrong tree.

I like to portray it like this. The work that I do on myself for myself is like the cake. God and I work on the ingredients, mixing together, and produce this beautiful lemony, butter pound cake. What my husband adds to my life is the icing. Icing makes a great cake, even more wonderful and delicious. Here's the key. I can eat cake without icing and still be really satisfied. I can't really eat icing without cake and have the same experience. It's sappy, sweet and not quite as satisfying. Queens, stop trying to fill up on icing. Your first work is with you and God alone. This allows you to love yourself and out of your overflow extend that same love to and with your husband.

Lines in the sand

As we navigate this area of unconditional love, we still have to set boundaries even in marriage. For more on this subject, check out Dr. Henry Cloud's books on it. Many times, some of the biggest problems in our relationships have to do with violations of boundaries or having unset boundaries. Other times, you have a boundary that you have not communicated so your King has no idea that he has crossed the line with you.

There have to be certain areas that you will not go. I'll give you an example. In our marriage, there will be no out-of-control, yelling, cursing matches. Besides the fact that that's not in line with my character as a woman of God, it's not something that I will allow in my life. I've never seen that in a home and will not allow my children to be exposed to that. Our boundary is that we will not have a discussion about any conflict until we can discuss it civilly. We take responsibility for our own self-control. Everything must go through the filter of agape love. I know we forget about it in the "heat of the moment" sometimes. That's why taking timeouts are a great idea. The Earth will not fall apart if you take a break and calm yourself down emotionally before you address a matter together.

"Teach A Wife" Tips

God desires for us to be happy. This happiness comes from living the law of love. Here's an action step to help you do just that. Get your Bible and turn to 1 Corinthians 13:4-8. This is a very familiar passage and is often known as the love chapter. As I said before, you are love. This is what we're going to do to remind ourselves of this truth on a daily basis.

Read the passage out loud daily. Everywhere you see the word love, put your name or "I" there. I have personalized it for you below.

"I am patient and kind. I refuse to be jealous or boastful or proud or rude. I don't demand my own way. I release irritability and will not keep record of being wronged. I will not rejoice about injustice, but I consistently rejoice whenever the truth wins out. I never give up, I never lose faith, I am always hopeful, and endure through every circumstance. Prophecy and speaking in unknown languages and special knowledge will become useless. But the love of God in me as me lasts forever!"

154

Here's part two. Substitute your husband's name for love and pray that prayer for him on a daily basis. Put it on a note card and keep it in your purse so that you can refer to it throughout the day. Put it on your car dashboard. Hang it on your mirror or on your refrigerator.

Make love your meditation, especially during difficult times. Think about how much God loves you and has forgiven you. Endeavor to live by that same law of love with your husband. It will allow you to be kinder. It will increase your level of patience. It will grow greater compassion in your heart for your Beloved.

What a "Ho" Can Teach A Wife

CHAPTER 11

Live Your Vows

If you want a successful marriage, learn to love and accept each other as you are.

It is the most glorious day you have ever seen. Your heart is bursting with excitement. Today you are getting married to the love of your life. Wow! It's finally here. The greatest care has been taken to adorn your ceremony like the fairytale dream you've been imagining all of your life. You have never felt more beautiful, and your Beloved is simply handsome and dashing in his tuxedo.

You turn to each other and say these words (or something similar).

"I, ___, take thee, ___, to be my wedded husband/wife, to have and to hold, from this day forward, for better, for worse, for richer, for poorer, in sickness and in health, to love and to cherish, till death do us part, according to God's holy ordinance; and thereto I pledge thee my faith [or] pledge myself to you."

Do you remember your vows? When was the last time that you even looked at them? Was it at your wedding? Are you living them?

Several years ago, I remember when these questions haunted me. Here's what happened. I was at an event called "Word to the Wives." It was given by Kristin Young of Living the Vows. At that time, I had been married for 17 years. I came to support a friend of mine who was the speaker at the event. Honestly, that was the only reason I was there, to support my Queen Sister. For real, I was a little tired of Brian at that time. OK, I'm minimizing it. I was a lot tired of Brian, but I came with an open mind to learn and to grow. Here's a key Queens. Keep an open mind and heart at all times. You never know who or what God will use to teach you. Some of my most powerful lessons were completely unexpected and from unusual sources.

During the event, when Kristin began to talk about living the vows I had to face myself.

I, Karin take you, Brian....

Stop right there. I felt sucker-punched from those words. It was as if time stood still. A huge mirror flashed before me and I saw myself. I realized that I was NOT taking him. It's funny because I didn't feel like I was really seeking, but I did find a jewel that transformed my life. Something deeper within me was seeking. I knew there was more, but I didn't know how to get there.

Queen, I hadn't even thought of my vows in so many years. I certainly had not been going back to look at them. They just were not top-of-mind. It wasn't that we flippantly got into this marriage. I shared with you our journey. We waited. We prayed. We believed God for each other. We studied the Word together. We did the premarital counseling. We got permission and the blessing of those who were authority figures in our lives. We read the vows. We had heard them dozens of times over the years, but we were not living them.

We were existing, passing the time, not dealing with our issues in a positive way, and not honoring the commitments that we made to each other and God in the presence of over 400 people. We were not walking in love with each other. In many ways, we were simply tolerating each other.

Personally, I had to come face-to-face with the truth about myself. In the process of trying to adjust to life with each other with all of the baggage that each of us brought, I'd stopped taking him. The only taking that I thought about was "I don't have to take this!" Now, let's be clear, of course, I am not talking about taking abuse. God is not into abuse and you shouldn't be either.

Here's what I wanted. I wanted to take his strengths, but didn't want to accept his perceived weaknesses. Yes, I wanted to take him when he was on the mountaintop, but I was not accepting of him in the valley of his doubts or fears. What happened to this person that I thought I was marrying? We all want Superman, but under the costume, under the masks, we also get Clark Kent. Clark Kent was the front that Superman put up so that he could blend in with society. What we often experience is the reverse. We see Superman out front. That's who we fall in love with. Many times, our men are afraid to show us who they really are and how they feel because society has villainized men for feeling or looking "weak."

Who said that you would never feel fear just because you're a man? Who said you always need to know which way to go and to have all the answers? Who said that you need to always be on top and never feel low or sad? Being in touch with your feelings is a strength, not a weakness. I didn't want to take Brian feeling unsure of himself, especially when in my own skewed perception of what a wife was supposed to be, I was supposed to follow him no matter what. He was in charge and was supposed to lead us. I was just supposed to listen and go along. No. I wasn't taking that.

There were things about him that I wanted him to change. "Why couldn't he be more like this? Why wouldn't he do more of that? I would feel better if he stopped doing this," I thought almost incessantly. What I didn't know was that I couldn't get "there" from here. I couldn't get to the happy marriage I wanted by expecting to feel happy only when all conditions were perfect.

Queen, you can't get to feeling better about your marriage or your life by waiting for the outside things to change. Here's one of my favorite verses on this with my own spin on it. Proverbs 15:15: "She who has a merry, cheerful, thankful heart, has a continual feast [aka a constant party, regardless of the circumstances]."

You must decide to have joy regardless.

I had to decide to grow up and love up, and a huge part of that meant loving and accepting Brian just as he was. Over the years, I have come to realize this. Men often marry us hoping that we will never change. They marry us based on how they feel about themselves when they are with us. They feel like The Man when they're with us. They feel like they can be our hero. They feel loved and respected. They feel like they can depend on us, that we have their backs.

Many times, women get married because we feel loved by our husbands. We feel safe with them. We feel protected by them. We feel like they will be there for us. We feel like they will be great providers. However, if we're honest, we're often hoping consciously or subconsciously that we can get into the relationship and change a few things about them. We look at them as somewhat raw ingredients that just need a wife to help them pull themselves together.

I've often heard women advise other Queens not to leave their marriages or relationships because "You've already put all of that work into him making him who he is and now you're going to let some other woman reap the rewards of your years of work?" It's almost as if we think we are supposed to mother our men. Now, if you've never heard that or you've never felt that way, great but it is extremely prevalent in the psyche of many women. We feel like we just need to fix them up a bit. I'll work on this more later.

But, is this a representation of agape love? Agape love is unconditional. It loves regardless of your faults and weaknesses. It honors and supports. It builds up and does not tear down. We forget during the worst seasons that we said we would take them during the worst seasons. When we are struggling financially, we don't remember that we said we take him when we go through a "poorer season." When we made those bold declarations, we didn't say, "…as long as the season doesn't last too long because you need to be bringing in enough money and make me feel safe at all times." Some of us are willing to hang with our husbands through a season of sickness, but what if it goes on for years and years? What if the sickness is not physical and it is mental illness? What if the sickness is in his soul or is emotional? He's plagued with low self-esteem or insecurity? He can't seem to break free from a victim mentality? He just doesn't know his value or think he's enough? Are we willing to be with him and to help him through those seasons? Will we love him and cherish him through all of that? Are we willing to stand in, depend on, and live through the love of God in those difficulties?

These are the vows that we made. Will you live them? In the core of his being, your husband wants a wife who will never give up on him, who will never give up on the two of you. Who will believe beyond hope. Who will trust God to fill in and to heal the broken places in him. Is that you?

"Teach A Wife" Tips

I know that I have said a lot. What are you going to do about this? I want you to pull out your vows. Read them. Meditate on them. Make it an assignment. Put them in a place where you can see them every day. Frame them and put them up in your family room. Voice-record yourself reading them and listen to it on a daily basis. Make some new vows and new commitments that you are willing to stand firmly on. Start small. Take it one step at a time. Pray and ask God to help you. You can indeed do all things through Christ who strengthens you. Lean on him. Live your vows.

161

What a "Ho" Can Teach A Wife

CHAPTER 12

It's What You Say and How You Say It: Dealing with Conflict!

Have you ever felt like your marriage could be so much better if you could communicate more effectively with each other, especially during conflicts? I know that's how I felt when Brian and I were going through it. Recently, I was reading an article in the Huffington Post that cited poor communications as the #1 cause of divorce. I believe it. If it's not #1, it is certainly high on the list of the greatest causes of distress and unhappiness in marriage because communication impacts all areas of our lives.

Let's say you thought your biggest problem had to do with finances. Somewhere along the line there's probably been some poor communication about how the finances should be handled and how to reach common ground on executing any financial plan together. That still involves communication. Even if you thought your biggest problem was sexual, that still involves communication. Are you unable to express your desires in the bedroom? Are you expecting your spouse to know how to please you when he has no idea how? Everything still points back to communication in one way, shape, or form.

I'd love to share with you a few points on creating healthy

communication with your King. This is part of what I tell my clients in my monthly wife support program called Queen Wife Mastery Membership. For more information on it, you can go to www.teachawife.com.

Speak from the first person

When you're communicating your feelings, always speak from the first person. Start with I, me, and my as opposed to you and your. Remember, this is about you. Your feelings are about you. When you say you, it makes it seem like you are making your husband responsible for your feelings. He's not. This is about how you are feeling. Be woman enough to own your feelings and to stand behind them. This is not the time to say you always do this or that. This is the time to say, "I feel (whatever feeling and/or emotion) when you do this or that." Not, you make me so mad when… No. You have chosen to be mad. There's a reason for it, but the choice to feel angry is yours. That is your interpretation, but you have a right to feel whatever you are feeling and to express how his actions feel to you.

This is sometimes difficult, especially in the heat of the moment. Do not communicate until you have grounded yourself. What do I mean by that? Make sure that you have taken time to pray, to meditate, and to get really clear on what you desire to say based on your own experience. How are you feeling? Why are you feeling that way? What does the situation remind you of? Are your feelings simply about this present situation or are you piling on some feelings from past situations too? Be really honest with yourself.

Here are a few things to keep in mind as you address any conversation about your feelings. Remember that you have nothing to prove. You really do not. You are simply sharing your feelings about the experience. You are not trying to convince or cajole him at all. You are just sharing. Also, you have nothing to defend. You do not have to get him on your side. You don't have to win anything. In fact, your goal is to leave any communication as win-win. Win-win means that both of you have been heard and at least accepted or understood. This is not a competition. This is not a fight to see who's right. Again, you can be happy or you can be right and sometimes you can be both. Think about your goal. It is ultimately to be able to create a common ground of understanding. Lastly, you have nothing to hide. Remember, your husband is not your enemy. In the spirit of love, you think the best of him. You don't have to hide who you are or how you feel. Assume love and acceptance. Expect him to want to hear you, to hear your heart. If you disarm yourself first before you start, then you can begin with a calm spirit and share from your perspective in an open and peaceful manner.

Pay attention to your patterns

Creating a space for healthy communication means that you must be willing to examine how healthy you are within. What patterns do you exhibit in your communication? In the past, I had a tendency of avoiding and convincing myself that things weren't a big deal. In reality, they were a big deal. You know how we get sometimes. We want to act like we are so above being bothered, but the truth is that we are so bothered and stuffing that frustration and anger inside. Have you ever done that?

Don't you know people can pick up on your energy? They know you've got an attitude even though you're smiling. Your husband is no different. He knows that your saying, "I'm fine" really means that you're not fine. He's wondering what he's done wrong now and you may be too cowardly to just share your feelings about what's going on in a way that we can hear it.

So, how do you show up? Be honest with yourself. Do you sweep things under the rug and suppress it. That's what I used to do. Why? Because I'm a minister, I had this false notion that if I were being

165

spiritually mature, then almost nothing is supposed to bother me. How about you? Have you swept so much stuff under the rug that it's now bigger than the rug? You can't hide it. You can't cover it. You think that no one can see all the mess that's spilling out. We can see it. It's spilling out all over your life, not just with your Beloved. It's spilling out with other family, with your friends, and at work simply because you won't be courageous enough to address the elephant in the room that we all see anyway. You wanted real talk, right? Here it is.

Are you exploding or imploding? Is that your pattern? Have you ever blown up a balloon and you knew it was getting close to being full, but you kept blowing anyway? What happened? It popped. That's what we do in our relationships. You just keep letting yourself get filled up more and more and more and more. You keep telling yourself, "He has one more time to do this. If he talks to me like that one more time" and then you pop. You go off. You're like a raging volcano that spews lava everywhere destroying whatever it touches. You're exploding. What would happen if you addressed your concerns right from the start? There would be a lot less negative energy built up. You would not have experienced the stress and frustration from trying to ignore it. Perhaps your Beloved doesn't even know that what he's doing is having that effect on you.

Maybe you're really like I was. You've held things inside for so long. Now the pain is too great and it's like an implosion takes place. It is just as destructive as an explosion but you get torn up inside. If you have ever lived in a metropolitan area, from time to time large buildings located right in the center of town need to be leveled. It's amazing to see how they're able to strategically place the explosives in the building and time the detonation so that the building collapses onto itself in just a matter of seconds. They implode buildings to minimize the damage to surrounding buildings. So here you are, pretending to be unbothered while internally blowing up and collapsing onto yourself while everyone else is walking around like nothing happened. But that's you, right? You have the responsibility of sharing your feelings

166

and expressing your concerns and letting your spouse know what's on your heart. Instead, your sense of self collapses on itself. You shut your own voice off. You deny your own desires because you won't stand up and speak up. Your husband is not your enemy. He loves you and wants the best for you. Open up your mouth and speak.

Here are some additional check points. In tough conversations, do you clam up or do you talk incessantly? Do you go off topic or do you stay focused? Do you listen or do you just wait for your time to talk? Are you loud and over-talking your man? Do you have a tendency to interrupt?

Here's a side note. Brothers find it so disrespectful to be interrupted. The thought is that if you ask them a question, then it must be important for you to hear their answer. When you don't even allow him to get an answer out, that feels disrespectful. It feels like you don't care about what he thinks or what he has to say. It feels like his thoughts don't matter to you. Do you allow your Beloved to speak his truth without being wrong? Can it just be? No judgment. No measuring up or down. These are just his thoughts.

Queen, please be gut-level honest with yourself about how you have been showing up so you can be aware. After awareness, there must be an adjustment. You must be willing to do your own work first. What destructive communication patterns do you have that you need to work on? Are you ready to change them? Only you can do that. This process that you go through will help you not just in your marriage, but in all of your relationships.

Do your own work first

Process your own pain. Where is this coming from? When have you felt like this before? Have you forgiven the person or situation from the past? If you haven't, you are more than likely causing your husband to pay for that past pain with you now. Do your own work Queen.

In times of conflict, my husband used to say that I acted like it was always about him. Honestly, I felt like it was mostly him. The only problem with that was that I was not humbling myself to acknowledge my part in the equation. Because of that, it did not invite him to step up to the plate to deal with his own issues. When people feel attacked, they most often will try to defend themselves. He's no longer hearing you because he's putting up a shield to keep you from hurting him. I had to realize this. Two wrongs don't make a right, but what's the goal? I'm only responsible for myself, but my shift allowed him to respond to my shift. I had to acknowledge that some of issues were from me and about me. I had accept that I have blind spots. What?! Yep. Sure do. And so do you.

Here's a big one. Accept that your King probably has a good reason for why he is doing what he is doing. It might not make sense to you or anyone else how he does it, but we must look at him through the eyes of love and believe that he is trying to come from a good place. Are you willing to give your man the benefit of the doubt? Be aware of this. He may not be expressing himself in a way that is beneficial, but there's a good reason. Often, we are just trying to protect ourselves in some way. We are trying to keep ourselves from being hurt.

Deal with your own anger first. Anger is not a sign that you need to communicate right now. It's a signal for you to go within and deal with what's going on in you. What needs to change? What's out of alignment? What do I need? Love yourself enough to not allow things to stack up to the point where you explode. If you are angry, sort your own stuff out first so that you can communicate with love instead of blame or resentment.

"Speak the truth in love…"
Ephesians 4:15

Speak the truth in love

Speaking the truth in love is grown folks' conversation. It takes nothing to simply go off on someone. Anyone can do that. It takes a mature person to stop and think before they speak. This is why I say that marriage will grow you up if you let it. Ask yourself, what is my motive for this conversation? Is my motive pure? Is it for love's sake? Am I trying to prove a point or am I trying to create more intimacy? Am I trying to understand as much as I am trying to be understood? Stephen Covey, author of "Seven Habits of Highly Effective People," encourages us to always seek to understand first. That is love in action. It is being able to drop the selfishness and allow yourself to walk in your spouse's shoes. Even if you can't fully do it, you actually try to see it from his perspective. You try to feel what he may be feeling. I will say it again. Your King is not your enemy. You're on the same team. Make sure that you are clear about what you want to say and why and that your words build up and do not tear down. In Proverbs 14:1, the scripture says that, "The wise woman builds her house, but the foolish pulls it down with her hands," or rather with her own mouth. Let your words edify, exhort, and comfort.

Complain without criticizing

A complaint is an expression of discontent, grief, or pain. Although I think there is great value in not being an incessant complainer, there are times when you do need to express something that has been unpleasant to you. If you've ever read Will Bowen's book, "A Complaint Free World," he states it along these lines. I'm putting it in my own words, but when we share something that is a discomfort for us and merely state the facts, that is not a complaint. When we add all kinds of negative emotion to our expression of this discontentment,

169

that's when it has rolled over into the complaint zone. You'll have to read his book to get the full monty on it. It's great.

I do feel like you need to give each other the space to be able to state a complaint. Remember, a complaint is about you. It is about your feelings and how you feel someone or something has had an effect on you. Criticism is a different animal. Criticism goes beyond complaint and attacks the character of your spouse. For example, perhaps your spouse keeps allowing the trash to run over onto the floor. Here's a complaint. "Honey, I'm starting to feel really frustrated about the trash running over on the floor. Would you please empty it? That really helps me to feel like we're maintaining order in the house together. Thank you, Love."

A criticism will sound something like this, "You always let the trash run over onto the floor. What's wrong with you? Don't you see that? Can you at least put the trash out? Do I have to do everything around this house?!"

Before you say that's an extreme example, I promise you that it is not. I have seen and heard women criticize and degrade their husbands in that way. And then they wonder why they're not connected. Your husband is not a child. Even children don't need to be demeaned. I hope you also saw in the complaint that I asked for what I would like and told why I wanted it done. Alison Armstrong puts it this way, "A critic is a chicken with a need." In other words, there's something that you need, but you are too chicken to ask for it, so instead you criticize and demean your King. That's a huge intimacy killer. It will shut your man down every time. State your complaint like it's just a fact. Remove the sting from it. Then ask for what you want and share why you want it. It really does work.

Pray and ask God to help you

When we pray, God answers. He's always right there with us. He says to call on Him, and He will answer and show us great and mighty things that we don't know (Jeremiah 33:3). There are situations that we face when we don't know what to do. God does. He knew that you would face it, and he also knows how to bring you out of it. Sometimes we are calling our girlfriends when we need to be calling on God. We need to have a heart-to-heart with the Father and allow Him to speak life into our spirits. If we're open, He will lead us into all truth. Your help is just a call away.

These are just a few of the practical tools for improving your communication with your King. I promise you that when you improve your communication, your marital happiness will rise. For more help in this area, check out my Queen Wife Mastery Membership at www.teachawife.com.

171

What a "Ho" Can Teach A Wife

CHAPTER 13

Happiness in Oneness

"And Adam said, This is now bone of my bones, and flesh of my flesh: she shall be called Woman, because she was taken out of Man. Therefore shall a man leave his father and his mother, and shall cleave unto his wife: and they shall be one flesh."

Genesis 2:23-24

Understanding and working to achieve marital oneness will help to lead you to marital happiness. We've all heard the scripture about, "Leave and cleave." It is sharing with us that God's intention for our marriages were for us to leave our families of origin and to cleave or become one with our spouses.

Here's the problem with the idea of oneness. Some of us have been told that in order to be one, the two of you must meld into this one new organism in which there are no longer differences between you. You think the same way. You act the same way. You finish each other's sentences. You basically become this one new person. If you were not spoon-fed this philosophy, good for you.

I have encountered too many women who think marital oneness means that they have to give up parts of who they are and what they believe to fit into their husbands' viewpoints on life. Not true. Marriage is a symphony, not just one note. It is one of life's most beautiful harmonies for goodness' sake. Now, can I be honest? This is something that originally my husband and I differed in our viewpoints so much. He too had been sold a bill of goods that marriage is the two becoming one where the individuals no longer exist to a certain degree. To that I say, "If both of you are the same, then one of you is unnecessary."

If both of you are the same, then one of you is unnecessary.

One of the mysteries of marriage is how the two of you come together bringing all of your similarities and differences to become one. This disappearing and melding act that we see portrayed is perhaps part of the romantic notions fueled by Disney and others. While you may know each other's thoughts and finish each other's sentences, you still exist as two distinct individuals who decide to become one in your aim and goals together, your view of your life, and in how you love each other.

In mentoring and coaching women, this is a very big concern. As women, sometimes it is very easy for us to disappear into our roles and to lose ourselves. We become so concerned with being the best wife, the best mom, and the best daughter that we forget to be our best selves. Marriage is not about you and your husband robotically fusing into a collective like a scene from Star Trek. It is the beautiful dance between two individuals giving and receiving, being flexible at times to create a symphony of life together.

Think of an orchestra. The brass horn does not sound like the flute. The cello does not sound like the drums. The piano does not sound like the violin. Yet, when they play together in concert, it produces a melodious sound. When they harmonize making their own sounds, they make resonate music. So how do we do this Queens?

"...by the grace of God I am what I am..."
1 Corinthians 15:10

Stop giving up your own uniqueness

First, in order to create beautiful marital oneness, you must stop giving up your uniqueness to fit in with your husband and his life. I'm certainly not discouraging you from flexibility in considering how you do things. I'm strictly focused on the "who." My guess is that your husband chose you, picked you out of all of the billions of women in the world because of who you were. He didn't choose you to become a carbon copy of him. He chose you because of the unique beauty that you are and possess. Besides, when we give up our uniqueness in an attempt to fit in to other people's viewpoint of life, we end up becoming resentful. We start to see ourselves as a victim, as if our husbands or someone is forcing this conformity upon us. The truth is that we have become our own victimizer.

Women are simply more malleable. We're much more willing to mold and to bend. That flexibility can be a great thing. It allows us to shift and make changes in ourselves or in how we are doing things in order to make things work. Sometimes this plasticity is beneficial. However, there is a thin line here that is easy to cross. This is why you have to be so clear Queen about who you are and what God has called you to do, and then remain true to that. Certainly the means for fulfilling your purpose may change and then unfold in ways that you hadn't imagined. We are always in a state of evolution spiritually, mentally, emotionally, and physically. Or at least we should be.

Here's my caution: You should never betray yourself, who you are, and what you believe in the core of your being for anyone. Not even your husband. Unless something that you are doing is morally and ethically wrong, why are you changing who you are, your life course, and who God made you to be to fit in? The question of purpose should have been settled before you got married. If it's afterwards, you were going to have to find a common ground.

One thing to keep a note in your mind on is this. The only thing in life that is constant is change. Both you and your husband will constantly change. They may be micro changes, but you are changing. Be who you are. Speak your truth. Live authentically. Be uniquely you at all costs. A woman who is sure of herself knows her worth and value. She is willing to stand for it, and in it. This Queen is a value to her husband, not a detriment. You must be courageous enough to take that step.

I speak as a woman who knows this very intimately. When God began to speak with me about starting Queens for Christ, my husband was not on board. He had a number of limiting beliefs about what being in ministry meant and the effect that it would cause on our relationship and our family. By this time, I had gotten so divinely discontented with how my life was going because of not fulfilling my own purpose that I had to make a decision to follow God and His voice above all else. It was very difficult, but I was willing to endure the discomfort to receive God's approval. I know that many may not agree with this stance, but I can't concern myself with that. I answer to God above everyone else. When my husband saw that I was determined to do what God told me to do and that I would no longer allow myself to stay stuck in Lodebar (I'll explain.), he eventually came around. Once he saw the impact that my ministering to women was having and that I finished what I started, he began to see the light. He had to deal with his own insecurities. I could not do that for him. That was something that he had to work out between him and God, just like I had to make a decision to step up and do what God told me to do.

Let's talk about Lodebar. 2 Samuel 9 recounts when King David tried to see if there was anyone left from the house or family of Saul that he could show kindness to for Jonathan's sake. He and Jonathan were like peas in a pod. They loved each other completely. He was devastated to see Jonathan die and wanted to show his love to anyone who was left from their family lineage. David's servant told him of a young man named Mephibosheth, who was Jonathan's son.

Here's the skinny on Mephibosheth. When he was five years old, his father, Jonathan, was killed in battle. Her nurse, fearing that the Philistines would kill her and his son too, fled with him to the royal residence in Gibeah. In the process, she dropped him and both of his feet became crippled (2 Samuel 4:4). He was then taken to Gilead, where he found refuge in Lodebar.

Lodebar actually means a place of "no pasture." It means a place of "no word." If we look at it contextually, it was a place where people who were forgotten were. It had to be a lonely place, where people who had been injured or harmed by no fault of their own merely existed. It was a place where purpose was not thriving.

That is exactly how I felt with regard to my own personal purpose. We both knew prior to marriage that I had a calling on my life. I had ignored it and ran from it for years. I had suppressed it while shaking pom-poms for everyone else for decades. Now was my time to step up. No one and nothing was going to stop me from doing that. I refused to any longer give up my uniqueness and who I was. The process of this taking a stand for myself and being authentically myself has created a strength and spiritual power in me that would have never been formed otherwise. Bottom line is this, you've got to follow God and be yourself. God will lead you in how, but be true to you. True to form, God will deal with your husband and give him wisdom in the process.

Appreciate your differences

Once you have gotten clear and totally secure in being who you are and expressing who you are, you must begin to appreciate your differences if you are to create marital oneness. Appreciate the different sound you each bring to the Earth. Honor each other's differences. Give attention to the contrast between you. Applaud the opposites. God made each of you to be who you are. You both bring a host of gifts to your marriage that will bless both of you. Learning to appreciate each other's differences allows you to see how they can be strengths for each other and your marriage.

I'll give you an example. Years ago, Brian and I attended Dave Ramsey's Financial Peace University. Dave talks about the two types of spenders that often end up with each other in marriage. The first is the Bubbling Brook and the second is the Dead Sea. The Bubbling Brook is the spender. They spend, spend, and spend some more, which can be an irritant to the Dead Sea. The Dead Sea experiences the Bubbling Brook as a spendthrift. It feels like they are constantly wasting money in an irresponsible way. That may not be true, but that's how the Dead Sea perceives it based on their lens of life.

The Dead Sea is the saver. They will squeeze a dollar until it hollers. They can be a tightwad. They might spend more time trying to get a deal instead of actually just getting what they want and enjoying it. This is perplexing to the Bubbling Brook, as it might feel like the Dead Sea needs to live a little. These two spenders can really bump heads with each other because their philosophies on how to use money is so very different. In our relationship, Brian is more like the Bubbling Brook and I am more like the Dead Sea. Although we are not extreme on either end, we're definitely closer to those ends. Dave explains that the Bubbling Brook allows you to have a life. If it weren't for the Bubbling Brook's liberality, the Dead Sea probably would not enjoy the experiences of life at all because they won't let go enough to do so. Conversely, the Dead Sea makes sure that you have anything to enjoy life with. If it weren't for the Dead Sea pulling the reins back from time to time, the Bubbling Brook would have you totally broke.

Get the point? Each of you has a point of view that is valid and brings strength to your union when you come together in appreciation of it. When you can acknowledge and welcome each other's different perspectives and points of view, you help to balance each other out. It is a sign of humility and maturity when you can accept that your point of view is not the only valid one. Decide to come together in unity with each other because of the richness of your differences and the fuller meaning that you can bring to life together.

The truth about irreconcilable differences

Irreconcilable differences is one of the most common grounds for divorce. It is the irretrievable breakdown of a marriage, meaning that you had differences that you could not overcome. I'm certainly not here to invalidate that as a means for divorce, but I am here to tell you that sometimes you will have to agree to disagree. This is unsettling for some people who feel that in order to be one there must be agreement at all times. Really?

This is a great place to share with you about one of my favorite authors and teachers on the subject of marriage, Dr. John Gottman. Dr. Gottman is an award-winning speaker, author, and professor emeritus in psychology. He is the foremost researcher on marriage stability and divorce prediction in the world, hands down, end of discussion. Please don't get religious here and tell me, "No. God is." As wonderful and complete as the Bible is, it does not give us all of the "how to do everything." Besides, God was talking before the Bible existed, and He is still talking now.

Dr. Gottman has researched marriages, up close and personal, for over four decades in what is known as the Marriage Lab at the University of Washington. He has been able to identify indicators of divorce and the components that lead to healthy and happy marriages. From their research, they can predict with over 90% accuracy how the conversation would progress, how happy the couple would be, and whether or not a marriage will lead to divorce within the next 5 years just from watching how a couple handles conflict for 15 minutes, if the destructive behaviors do not change. I'd say those are pretty good statistics. I tell you a little snippet of his resume so that you can get this truth about irreconcilable differences.

From Dr. Gottman's research, he has found that 69% of all couples' conflicts are unsolvable conflicts. Do you hear that? These conflicts are unsolvable because they have to do with differences in your personalities that constantly create conflict or they are from fundamental differences in your individual lifestyle needs. These conflicts lead to what he terms perpetual problems. In his research, they conclude that instead of trying to solve the perpetual problems, what seems to be most important is trying to establish a dialogue about them. Here's how I would phrase it. If you are not able to simply understand and accept each other in that perpetual problem area, an impasse is created and will lead to emotional disconnection.

There are times when we just have to accept that's just who he is. He's probably not going to change that, and I will not allow my love for him to change as a result of it. I accept my King as he is even if I don't agree with what he does. Wait, there's more.

Dr. Gottman says that the average happy couple had 7-10 unresolvable conflicts. Do you hear that? I think that we may have three or four untouchable subjects where we reach an impasse in our communication and we feel like our marriages are doomed. That's not true. It is all in how you see it. Perception is everything. Trust that there is nothing wrong with your marriage because you have irreconcilable differences. It is absolutely normal to experience challenges when two different people with two different backgrounds come together to create one mission for a marriage. This was extremely liberating for me. It let me know that I was not alone and that I could still have a happy marriage without "coming into agreement" about everything and solving every conflict.

Sometimes, we try to force an issue because we get so caught up into thinking that conflict is wrong. It is not. It is to be expected. But, we can disagree without becoming disagreeable. We are supposed to be different. You are very different even if you both love Jesus and His Word. I repeat, if both of us are the same, then one of us is not necessary. We're together because we are different. We may be alike in terms of our spirit and things that we share that brought us together. Yes, like attracts, but the things that hold us together and cause us to grow together are those differences that will help and supply a need in each other. Honor that!

Grab your Queen Wife Journal.

It's time for some reflection. Take time to think about the differences that you and your husband have. How do you balance each other out? What are the qualities that you admire about him? What does he do that you would never be able to do? Where does your King hold you up? How do you do the same for him? Appreciate the dance. Really think about it. Those differences make you brilliant together, and appreciating them brings power to the dynamics of your love.

What a "Ho" Can Teach A Wife

CHAPTER 14

You Can Only Change Yourself

Queen, hear me. Let me say this loudly and clearly. You can only change yourself, so stop trying to change your husband. You can be his wife or his mama. Last I checked, most men don't want to make love to their mothers, and if yours does, you need more help than my book here can provide you. If that's what's up, stop and get to your closest minister of deliverance, psychologist, or family counselor now. My love, my Sister, you can only change you. This is so simple and yet we violate it so often.

I mentioned in the first part how a lot of times men get married because of how they feel about themselves when they are with you. They feel loved. They feel respected. They feel accepted. They feel like The Man. They feel like they can make you happy. They wish that you would never change.

We, on the other hand, sometimes feel like, "Oh, he's wonderful, but I'm just going to have to work on that little part there." If you are like me, you were told that men are often like raw materials and that you'll just have to work on them a little bit to get them like you want them. Somehow inside of us ladies, Queens, we feel like it's our responsibility to fix him up a bit. Dust him off some. Make him who he "needs" to be.

Now the truth is we ALL need to grow and change. Additionally, we both want to support one another in our own growth and change.

However, we cannot make anyone change. It is a recipe for disaster in any relationship and especially in marriage. The moment that we start letting our husbands know that we think there is something wrong with him and we need to point it out to them, we are heading down a slippery slope. Ask me how I know? Wrote the book. Wrote the screenplay. Starred in it. Won the Oscar. Trust me on this one. I know.

The Four Horsemen of the Apocalypse

Dr. John Gottman, in his brilliant work, shares what he calls the "Four Horsemen of the Apocalypse" in marriage. They are the signs of inevitable doom to love and intimacy in marriage that can and often do lead to eventual divorce. I will share them here, and I want you to see if you have been doing these in your marriage, because if you are, it is time to change yourself and what you are thinking, feeling, believing, and doing. He describes these Horsemen and what you can do about them as the difference between the masters in relationship and the disasters in relationship.

1. Criticism

The first horseman is criticism. We shared on this earlier in the book, but because it is of such great consequence, it bears repetition. Offering a complaint is different than criticizing. With a complaint, you are expressing displeasure, and it is about how you feel and what you need. A criticism is an attack on your husband's character. It is a charge against who he is.

A complaint would be, "Honey I feel disappointed when you don't call me to say that you won't be home for dinner when I've taken time to prepare something special for you so we can connect over dinner. I thought we agreed that you would call beforehand. Could you please at least call to let me know if you won't be home?"

184

A criticism is, "You never think about the fact that I have slaved over this stove after I've worked all day to make something for you. And you don't even call me to tell me you're not coming! You are so thoughtless and insensitive!"

Complain without criticizing

See the difference? Criticism is making a character assassination, and it never works. It is often used to make your position right and their actions wrong. From your husband's point of view, it feels like you are pointing the finger at him and tearing him apart in order to show him what's wrong with him. Can you see how this is an enemy of intimacy? It's difficult to feel close to someone when you feel like the person sees you as the one in the relationship who is causing all of the problems. Instead of criticizing, discuss your feelings and simply ask for what you want in a loving way.

When criticism is a constant in your marriage, what often happens is it leads to the next horseman. It becomes pervasive. Anything that you focus on only gets bigger. You will find more problems issues and concerns to magnify and countless things to criticize.

2. Defensiveness

The second horseman is defensiveness. We can all get defensive from time to time, but if your marriage is in trouble, it's almost always there. Why do we get defensive? When we feel attacked, we want to defend ourselves or protect ourselves from injury. We get defensive so that our spouse will leave us alone, but it doesn't work.

Here's how this may play out. You might ask, "Babe, did you take care of paying the bills like you said you would?" and he defends with, "Well, I was just so busy at work doing everything and you got home before I did. Why didn't you take care of it?"

He smells a fight coming on and he's ducking to make sure that you don't hit him with the criticism that seems to be coming inevitably. Then, not only is he becoming defensive about your question about what he didn't do, but then he's trying to make you wrong. Masters in relationships take responsibility for themselves. They own up to their part in conflict. What would've been better is, "Oops. No. I didn't take care of that. Let me do it right now." What can happen when we are focused on negative communication is that we are so conditioned to be armored up that it becomes an automatic reaction to defend ourselves, regardless of how inappropriate the defense is.

What do we do about that? What do we do when our King is being defensive even when you are not trying to attack him? Please know, if this is happening, there's somewhere perhaps in your relationship where he has felt attacked, he's lived through women in his life prior to you that attacked him consistently or he attacks himself. He's gotten used to the poison of self-criticism and he's just defensive in life. I certainly don't want to say that every problem that you all are having in your relationship is just about the two of you. Often it is not.

"Do not let your adornment be merely outward— arranging the hair, wearing gold, or putting on fine apparel rather let it be the hidden person of the heart, with the incorruptible beauty of a gentle and quiet spirit, which is very precious in the sight of God."

1 Peter 3:3-4

Go soft

What do I do with that? Go soft. "SOFT!" you might think, "If I go soft then I will have nothing to protect myself." That's right. Nothing

186

in the natural. But we must understand that God is a shield about us. This is where you're going to have to rely on 1 Peter 3:4. It says that a wife with "a meek and quiet spirit is of great price." Ladies, we must soften.

Keep this in mind. Your husband spends all day fighting the world. He doesn't want to come home and fight you too. We must create a soft space for them to land. And yes, you catch more bees with honey. We must choose to believe that if we speak the truth in love and watch our tongues then God will be with us. As you soften, it softens his heart. Remember how we said that Moses permitted divorce because of the hardening of men's hearts? Your softness will soften his heart.

"A soft answer turns away wrath, but a harsh word stirs up anger."

Proverbs 15:1

Watch your tone

Do you speak gently? Is there a softness to your words and your tone? Tone is extremely important to men. Sometimes the tone is far more important than even what you are saying. Here's an experience that I had in this area to help you see my point. It was Christmas. I emphasize that because it is often a very stressful time of the year for both me and my husband. I used to feel really stressed because it seemed like everything fell on me for the holidays, and I do mean everything. Brian was always super busy with catering holiday parties at work. This is a preface to give you framework because we were both a little on the edge.

I was on a course of treatment in which my naturopathic doctor had me taking Chinese herbs that were in tablet form and making them into a tea. I took my tablets, made my tea, and set it on the counter to drink later. I came down to the kitchen, and my husband

187

was putting my teacup into the dishwasher. "Why'd you pour out my tea!" I exclaimed. I realize it wasn't a question. I knew he had done it. I was merely wondering why he was messing with my teacup. He looked at me aghast. He replied, "I was just trying to straighten up the kitchen." Feeling exasperated, I just left the room, but there was an icy silence between us. As I was sitting in my office, I heard the word "Luther."

Mistranslation

Who's Luther? I'm about to tell you. I don't even know how I discovered Luther; perhaps someone shared it on Facebook, but Luther is the character from Key & Peele who plays President Obama's Anger Translator. If you've never seen it before, Google it. It is hilarious. The whole premise of the sketch is to show what Obama says to the public versus how pissed off he feels about the public. It shows how we as people can feel certain raging emotions inside of us but are able to couch our speech and expressions in a more palatable way.

The Holy Spirit tapped me on the shoulder and let me know that instead of Brian hearing me say, "Oh no! Why'd you pour out my tea?" he had heard, 'OH NO! WHY'D YOU POUR OUT MY TEA!!" He had heard it much to the extreme as Luther the Anger Translator sounds in contrast to what the character playing Obama is saying. It took me immediately back to the words of Dr. John Gray. Dr. John Gray has been around for decades, and his transcendent work on relationships should be followed as well. I had been listening to a talk that Dr. Gray did. He said this: If you do not communicate with your Beloved with a tone that says "happy and delight," men will inevitably mistranslate it.

Agape love is giving someone what they need, even if you don't.

188

It might not have been my intention to wound him. I was just annoyed that he'd poured out my tea, but in his mind, he felt attacked in some way. It was a mistranslation. That experience made me acutely aware of my tone. My husband used to say to me, "Can you put more "honey" into it?", meaning my speech. And then he would repeat back to me whatever my statement or question was with the "honey" in it that he was referring to. Inwardly, this made me want to roll my eyes out of the sockets. Real talk. Put more "honey" into it? Why? I felt like he didn't put "honey" into any requests for me. Here's where I had to grow up a bit in love. Agape love is giving someone what they need, even if you don't. I'm pretty straight. I can take it straight up no chaser. What's the big deal? The big deal is that's what he needed.

Consciously communicate

Queen, be conscious of your communication. Be gentle. Understand that your man can't take it like we can. It's true. This may seem odd because society would lead you to believe that men are like Clint Eastwood's characters, the strong silent type that nothing affects. Nothing could be farther from the truth when it comes to you. Although they may be able to take barbed wires out in the world, their hearts and minds are extremely sensitive to the speech and tone that we use with them. Extremely sensitive. They are conditioned to hide it in so many ways, but aren't you glad that people like Dr. Gray pull back the curtains to tell us what's really going on.

Be mature in conflict

As Dr. Gottman confirms, the masters in relationship are very gentle with one another. We see problems as something that we go after together. Assume the best of your spouse. Assume that he didn't mean to hurt you. Even when he seems to be attacking you, the mature response would be, "That's interesting. Tell me more." Refuse to take the bait of offense. When it's your turn to share something that he may not perceive positively, gently explain to him your feelings and what you need from him. In addition, accept your King's point of view, whether you agree with it or not. That's inconsequential. Take responsibility for your part in any conflict, and if you know that you need to apologize, do it.

3. Contempt

The third horseman is contempt. The intention of contempt is to insult or abuse your spouse. When criticism escalates into contemptuous behavior, it is often marked by disrespect, sarcasm, ridicule, mocking, and by body language such as eye rolling and exasperated gasps. In contempt, you are approaching your spouse from an air of superiority. You speak down to your man like you're better than him.

Here's an example. Contempt is when you say things like, "Oh so you get to sit around and watch the game all day while I get to clean the house, take care of the kids, make the meals, and work a job. I'm the only person who should be getting a break around here. What are you doing?" The criticism has gotten so bad that you just go straight for the jugular. The only problem is you're cutting his throat and all of the lifeblood of your marriage is seeping out with each dagger like words out of your mouth.

Culture of appreciation

What do we do about this? Understand this, contempt arises when you have long-standing resentment because of not addressing or dealing with your issues in a healthy way. Not surprisingly, it is also the single-greatest predictor of divorce. When you can't see any good in your spouse, it's over. It's just a matter of time. The remedy for this is developing a culture of appreciation for each other. We talked about it in appreciating your differences earlier in the book. Dr. Gottman states that for every negative comment, your spouse needs at least five positive comments in order to neutralize the effect of the negative one. I have read research that puts that ratio at 8 to 1 (eight positive comments to every one negative comment). Whatever the ratio really is, one thing is for sure, if we are going to have hot, holy, happy marriages, the thoughts, feelings, beliefs, words, and actions that we have toward ourselves, our spouses, and our marriages must intentionally be overwhelmingly more positive than negative.

You have power over your own positivity. You get to decide what you will think about. Just because a thought flies over your head or through it, you don't have to let it build a nest in your mind. You can let it pass right through. You can swat it away. You can replace low thoughts with higher thoughts. Every day, intentionally focus on what you appreciate about your husband. You chose him for a reason. Start to focus on that. Make yourself a daily list of "Things I Love About My King." If that's difficult, go back to when you did feel love and appreciation for him. Read that list daily. You've got to create a culture of appreciation about your Beloved if you are going to have the marriage you desire. You will have to change yourself in that area.

4. Stonewalling

The fourth horseman is stonewalling. Men often do this more than we do. Stonewalling is when the listener, your husband, withdraws from all interaction. He emotionally checks out. He is shutting himself down and closing himself off from you. The stonewalling is his way to tune out. When your partner stonewalls, you know it. It is evident in their body language. They don't give the usual cues that they are listening to you or picking up what you're putting down. Their body is closed off. Their head may be down. Their arms might be crossed. They're staring up at the ceiling and not looking you in the eye. In these instances, the stonewaller has become really upset and they're often stonewalling in an attempt to calm themselves down. What he may often be thinking is, "She'll eventually burn herself out." Or if you're the one stonewalling, you might be thinking, "just a few more minutes until I have to take the kids out and I'll be free. I'll just ignore him". Ouch! I've done that.

Dr. Gottman found that the husbands were often trying to keep from saying anything for which they'd be in more trouble for later. I have found this to be true. Men often feel like they are constantly in trouble. They feel that no matter what they do, we wives never seem happy. When a man does not know how to make you happy, eventually many will give up trying. It is more devastating for him to keep trying and failing than to not try at all.

The power of support

What do you do? This may be hard to hear, but it's true. You must work on changing yourself. Remember, you can only change YOU! You pray and ask God to show you your own heart. How can you shift how to talk to your husband so you can show love and respect for him? Ask your husband how you can support him.

For instance, let's just say that he didn't do something that he said he was going to. How do you approach it? Try this. "Honey I know that you said you were going to find a financial planner for us to meet with. Is there anything that I can do to help support you in that?" Here's why this works. It lets him know that you're still remembering that he hasn't done it yet. However, you're not berating him for not doing it. Then, you're asking how you can support him.

Having our support means the world to them. A good man does want to be held accountable. A straight-up Brother will allow you to lovingly remind him of who he is and what he said he would do to and for you. But, all Brothers are sensitive to how we do it.

Even if you didn't say it, you said it

Watch the 93%. How do you communicate verbally and non-verbally? Write this on your heart. Years ago, a study was done that stated that only 7% of our communication is words. Conversely, 93% is how we say it – our tone, volume, pitch, facial expressions, and other body language. While the study has been mildly refuted in recent years, the truth remains. Most of what you communicate is not the actual words. Your words are important, but how you say what you say is way more important. Pay attention to yourself and what you may be inadvertently communicating nonverbally. Even if you didn't say it with words, you said it.

Time-out

Take a break. When you sense that either or both of you need to cool off, take a break. There is no reason why you have to fight like cats and dogs through any interaction. Allow cooler heads to prevail. When you perceive a physical or emotional threat, i.e. you are extremely upset or stressed, you go into what is called fight, flight, or freeze. Adrenaline and cortisol are released into your bloodstream. Your heartbeat elevates. Your senses are heightened. Your blood is directed away from your brain and toward your limbs as if you are about to run from a saber-toothed tiger. You're ready to flee or you're ready to duke it out till the end. The third response is when you feel like your situation is hopeless and you freeze, like a deer in headlights. You're more willing to simply give up on things in a negative way. You do nothing, you say nothing, or you simply just disengage. None of these foster beautiful intimacy.

Take a time-out. Go and pray. Go for a walk. A little fresh air and deep breathing does wonders for centering yourself. Get your mind right. Remind yourself of the truth, because your ego, your carnal mind, will inevitably be trying to convince you of lies. Pull yourself together and reconvene. When you start again, acknowledge your error. Say something like, "Baby, I could see that things were not going in a positive fashion. I'm sorry for hurting your feelings. Let me explain what I'm really feeling."

Inspiring change in him

You can't make your King change, but you can inspire him to change. "Inspire" comes from a Latin word that means to "breathe into." It is thought of to mean "in Spirit" or "God-breathed." I certainly believe that God can breathe into us ways to effect change in our husbands. I love the work of Alison Armstrong. Like Dr. Gottman, she has been studying relationships for decades and is a leader in the field of understanding men, understanding women, and making relationships work. When it comes to men, she notes that almost nothing is worth doing but everything is worth providing.

How do we inspire our men to change? We do so by calling on one of their most instinctive, primal drives: the need to provide. By nature, men are providers. If you stumble across a Brother who is not interested in providing safety, security, and happiness for a woman, put him back in the oven; he's not fully baked yet. We will talk much more about that in the next chapter. They delight in providing. Let me share a quick story from what I learned from Alison.

Here is how we can inspire change in them. Very simply and lovingly ask for what you want and explain what it would do for you and how it would make you happy. This sounded way too simple to work, but I decided to test it out myself. We have been living in our house for over 12 years. My office is in the basement. Although it has decorator carpet and beautifully painted walls, the window still had the temporary stick-up paper blinds that people have on their windows when they first move into a house. Did I mention it's been over 12 years? The blinds were right in the house, but for some reason, my husband saw no need to put them up. I had read in Dr. Gary Chapman's book to let your man know what you want and that there was no need to repeat it. He already knew. Well, that didn't work for this Brother. He knew it but did nothing else about it.

I decided to give Alison's approach a swing. I went to my husband in my sweetest voice and said, "Honey, do you know what would make me so happy? I would love it if you could put those blinds up in my office for me please. Then I could regulate the amount of light that comes into the window and it would just be a much better, polished look and feel to the space. That would make me really, really happy." That was it. What happened next was nothing short of a miracle. Within less than 30 minutes, he was downstairs looking at the blinds that I had purchased. He figured out that they weren't going to fit. He went to Home Depot and picked out blinds that were much better than any blinds I would have picked out. He came home and put those blinds up the same day in my office window. Bam! Anytime I have used that approach, it has always worked. When our men know what would make us happy, and we express it to them in a loving way, it does indeed inspire them to change, to move, or to make things happen. Now don't forget this. Make sure you lavish him with love and appreciation after he does it if you want that behavior to continue.

Grab your Queen Wife Journal.

I know that this chapter may have been a little bit of castor oil. It doesn't taste so good going down, but it's good for you. Be honest with yourself. Do you see yourself in any of those Four Horsemen of the Apocalypse? Are you ready to shift those areas of your life and your marriage? I say life because these conflict styles probably are bleeding over into other relationships too. Write down where you are, but write down where you are believing God to take you. Reread each section and take the antidotes to heart. Practice them. Practice makes progress. Step by step, day by day, your King will see the changes in you and will respond. Your change will elicit a change in him. Be committed.

CHAPTER 15

He Wants to Please You

"When a man has taken a new wife, he shall not go out to war or be charged with any business; he shall be free at home one year, and bring happiness to his wife whom he has taken."

Deuteronomy 24:5

Honey hush! When I read this scripture in Deuteronomy, I was like, "I haven't ever heard anybody preach on this. Can y'all teach this at the Men's Conference?" Think of the marriages that would be transformed if a couple could just take a whole year to totally focus on each other and that man could put all of his energy into bringing happiness to his wife. Mind-blowing.

Even though your King may not have a whole year off to exclusively focus on pleasing you, your husband really does want to please you. You just must tell him how to. Now, this may seem hard to believe if you are in a difficult time in your relationship. The truth is, when a man loves a woman, there is nothing that makes him happier than to see you happy. There is nothing that makes his chest stick out more than to feel like he brings a smile to your face. He gets great joy and delight from knowing that being with him makes your heart skip. He feels like The Man!

Men are fixers

Have you ever noticed how when you tell your husband that something's wrong that he is automatically trying to see how to fix it? Even if something keeps him from actually fixing it, the wheels in his mind are turning. Men are fixers by nature. You identify a problem, they are looking for ways to fix it, especially if it means that it will please us.

Sometimes they don't understand that we often just need to talk about stuff just to get things out of us. What I want you to consider is that they are always looking to fix things to make things better for us. His thought is, "How can I take the stress off of her? How can I keep her from feeling sad?" Now, if your man is not doing this, more than likely, something has happened to prevent this.

They are not us

Again, men really want to please us. We just have to tell them how to do it. We sometimes look at men as if they are hairier versions of us. We think that they should know what we think. "He's seen me do this again and again, he should know what I like. If he loved me, he would… If he cared, he would have…. He should just pay attention to me. That's what I do."

I promise you. Men do not think the way that we do. As women, we are like gatherers. Men are like hunters. As gatherers, we are constantly gathering information. Security is an inborn need for women. Instinctively, we feel safer by doing more of what is pleasing and less of what is displeasing.

If you come over my house for tea and you say, "Oh I love to have honey in my tea and just a little bit of milk please," my brain

198

automatically notes it. That's what a feminine brain does naturally. Because of that, the next time you come over my house, I will remember the kind of tea that you liked, and I will have honey and milk in my fridge just for you.

Men do not gather like that. We think that it is insensitive and uncaring. Their brains do not work that way naturally. They are, as Alison Armstrong calls them, "hunters." Remember Queens, we are the ones who are into details. We function that way because we have greater communication between the left and right hemispheres of our brains. They do not. So, if you want your man to do something for you, you have to explain it explicitly. You need to tell him what you would like and in a way that he can receive it. I mentioned before that to a man, almost nothing is worth doing. They are masters of energy conservation—something that we need to learn more of as women.

We are the busy bees going, doing, noticing everything, and trying to take care of all things in the world. We are multitasking with the spinning plates. Men, by and large, get a goal in mind and they go after it. They finish that goal and they go on to the next one. That is why when your husband comes home, he comes in and puts the stuff down and he is relaxing on the couch. His goal is to relax.

Unless he is a caterer like my husband, he might not even see the dishes. The laundry piling up evades his attention. The same goes for the things that need to be picked up off of the floor. He has one goal in mind. The goal is to come home, relax, and unwind from the day. While your man is more singularly focused, we are often the ones who are running around like a chicken with its head cut off, stressed out, and overwhelmed. If we were more singularly focused too, we could probably eliminate 80% of our stress. So remember, it's not that your husband is being uncaring. He sort of sees things around the house, but he doesn't see it unless it is a part of the goal he's focused on at the moment.

"Ask, and you will receive, that your joy may be full."

John 16:24

You better ASK

The other thing about this difference between us and our men is this: Unless you ask or say something, they assume that you are OK. Listen honey, you better A-S-K if you want to G-E-T. The Scripture tells us to ask and we shall receive. Isn't it interesting that even God, who knows what we need before we even do, wants us to ask in order to receive, and yet, we just expect our men to know what we need, when we need it, and don't feel like we should have to ask them for anything?

Somewhere down on the inside of many women's souls is a fear of asking. Whether it comes from a fear of rejection, it is present. Maybe you've been listening to a voice inside of you that says you are too little, you're too much, it's impolite to ask, how dare you, why can't you just be satisfied with what you have, or some other variation. It's time to shut its mouth completely.

For most men, we seem like a moving target. In actuality, we often are. Depending on where you are at what time of the month, you are a different woman. Your hormone levels change, and they change you. It may be subtle, but it is noticeable. If you want certain things in your life from your Beloved, go ahead and settle this right now. Unless he completely knows, and even if you do think that he does, you had better ask for it. Ask lovingly and clearly. They are not the best at inference and subtle hints. They just aren't.

Who's going to do what?

When it comes to having a happy household, one of the biggest bones of contention in marriage is with the division of labor. Let me tell you how I had to learn this lesson about asking. Again, I saw a mother who worked outside of the home full-time and then came home and handled everything. I do mean everything. My father did little to nothing around the house and perhaps one or two things outside in the yard. This was his culture. He grew up with maids and servants in the West Indies, which is pretty accessible even on a modest income. He did not have to do those things. That was seen as work for women and servants. I cringe to think that that's how he looked at that. My mother, on the other hand, grew up on a farm. She was used to working and doing things.

My husband grew up with a mom who was basically a socialite. My husband was also accustomed to his mom handling everything at home. His father was a very busy entrepreneur, professor, and community leader. He was almost never home, so his mom had to handle almost everything.

Now for me, this was a recipe for disaster. I guess in my "nouveau thinking," I began to ask, "Why is it that I get to go to work full-time, mind you at the same place with my husband, and then have to come home and clock into a second full-time job?" This was not good for me. This went on for years before I even said anything because my paradigm told me that was what a "good wife" was supposed to do.

One day, I got the courage to ask why he never did more around the house to help, and it was so telling. My husband told me that because I never asked for help, he thought I was OK. What? I just assumed that he could see all the work that I was doing around the house in addition to taking on most of the parenting while working full-time outside of the home and that he would just know he needed to do more to assist. Nope. We sometimes expect our husbands to be mind readers. I'm going back to the Disney notions again. You have to ask for what you want.

Remember my story about the blinds? I had been waiting for Brian to put up those blinds in my office for 12 years. He got it done the same day when I changed how I asked for it. So again, for men, almost nothing is worth doing. They are extremely efficient beings. But, so much is worth providing. A man, a real man, provides and protects. When a man knows what you desire and what would make you really, really, happy, he will stop at almost nothing to provide it.

Remember the formula

Here is the formula again. Let your husband know exactly what would make you really, really, happy. Then let him know what it would provide for you. Make sure you let him know how much you appreciate him. You must say it all in a tone that expresses joy and delight. This has been one of the single-most game changers in my marriage. I have been able to lovingly communicate my desires and see them taken care of quickly almost every time when I do this.

I'll give you another story. I have never been to Hawaii. I told my husband how much I would really, really love to go to Hawaii. I explained to him that it would make me so happy to spend time together on that beautiful island relaxing and just enjoying each other on a long, kid-free vacation. My husband, who plans no trips, unbeknownst to me immediately got online and started researching packages. He had narrowed it down to one that he really liked and was going to surprise me. In the meantime, I decided that we should talk about putting the girls in private school. That's when I found out what he had been planning. We haven't gone yet, but he built up so many points just by stepping out and starting to plan it. Now, whenever I bring something up, he is almost immediately right on it. I'm telling you. It works!

The difference between the Masculine and the Feminine

By nature, men in their masculine state are givers, producers, and directive. Women, in our most feminine state, are receivers, nurturers, and multipliers. We also produce and give, but at our best, it is after we have received. If you look at your physiology you will see that is true. Men are givers. Women are receivers. We receive the seed, multiply it, and grow it into something way more than what it could've ever been without our feminine power on it. Give us a house, we will give you a home. Give us groceries and we will produce a fantastic meal. Give us a seed and we will give you a baby.

A good man finds joy in giving, producing, and directing. When what he gives to you or produces for you makes you happy, it is his delight. Ask and you shall receive so that your joy may be full. Let your Beloved know your desires in an honoring way and he will get to work to bring you joy.

It's Queen Wife Journal time.

Take some time to think about all the ways that your husband brings joy to your heart, a smile to your face, and a skip in your step even if you have to go way back into the memory bank. Beyond that, what would make you feel really happy right now? What are some of the things that you would love to do with your man? Take a moment to write them down. Write how you will ask him for your heart's desires. Get in front of the mirror and practice. Start small. It might work for you right away, or he may be thinking, "What's going on with her?" Stay at it. Men are hungry for appreciation.

CHAPTER 16

Submission: What It Is and What It's Not

Submission has become like a four-letter word to many women inside and outside of the church. It conjures up visions of domineering men who take advantage of women. It also makes you think of weak, mealy-mouthed women who allow themselves to be dominated and controlled. I promise you that submission the way God intended is neither. If you are to have a happy marriage, you're going to have to face this subject head-on. Let's look at the Word on the matter.

"Submitting yourselves one to another in the fear of God. For wives, this means submit to your husbands as to the Lord. For a husband is the head of his wife as Christ is the head of the church. He is the Savior of his body, the church. As the church submits to Christ, so you wives should submit to your husbands in everything. For husbands, this means love your wives, just as Christ loved the church. He gave up his life for her to make her holy and clean, washed by the cleansing of God's word. He did this to present her to himself as a glorious church without a spot or wrinkle or any other blemish. Instead, she will be holy and without fault. In the same way, husbands ought to love their wives as they love their own bodies. For a man who loves his wife shows love for himself. No one hates his own body but feeds and cares for it, just as Christ cares for the church. And we are members of his body."

Ephesians 5:21-30

Well. Well. Well. We're off into one of the most contentious and controversial subjects in marriage: submission. I say this with complete honesty, the church has certainly jacked this up royally along with the insecure ideologies of some of our Brothers and perhaps some of our Sisters too. Ready to dive in?

Here's what submission is not

Submission does not mean that you no longer have a right to your opinion or point of view. I have heard people teach that you must simply submit to your husband even when you know something is wrong and by the act of your submission, God will make it right. Really?

Submission is not blind unquestioned obedience. It does not mean that you just have to go along to get along and you just need to keep your mouth shut.

Submission is not that your husband gets to be a ruling tyrant making unilateral decisions and you have no say or ability to be involved in them.

Submission does not mean that your husband is superior or stronger or smarter or better at leading than you in any way. In fact, I have heard many Brothers say that their wives are much better leaders and pastors than they are.

Submission does not mean that you have to agree with every decision that is made either. How about that?

I have heard each of these taught or implied and so much more.

Let's look at what the word submission actually means.

Definition of Submission

It is the action of yielding to the force or to the will or authority of another person. It means "to defer to another's judgment, opinion, decision, etc."

Submission is a voluntary act, I repeat. It is a voluntary act of yielding to the authority or will of another. Here's the part that is not taught as often. Submission is something that goes both ways because you are both ultimately submitted to God. Ephesians 5 begins the conversation on submission by saying that we are to "submit ourselves one to another in the fear of God."

What that tells me is before anybody needs to start talking about that we need to submit to them, the question becomes are you first submitted to God? Are you listening to God's voice? Are you hearing and obeying what He is saying to you? Are you yielding to His authority, His judgment, and His decisions in your life? If not, please don't ask me or anyone else to submit to you. Just my thoughts. Let's move on.

Look at the word again and break it down. "Sub" means under or below. "Mission" means "assignment, goals, or purpose."

Now Queens, I know that there are women, who have a problem with submission. When it comes to issues with submission with men, it could be because they have been hurt and disappointed by men, starting with their own fathers. They could have experienced abandonment, abuse, and neglect, and are having difficulty with trusting men and probably people in general too. This lack of submission could be spilling over into all relationships with authority figures.

Can we go real talk here? Most of the Queens that I have encountered however do not really have a big problem with submission. They have a problem with getting under "no mission." Their issue is following someone, their husband, who is not showing leadership for them in a mission or assignment from God for them to support.

Now, this is my opinion. Most women don't have a problem with submission to the degree that it is spoken of. We are the great supporters of every cause that exists. If women all over the world dropped mics and exited stage left out of corporations, every economy would collapse under the weight of it. I think Beyonce might be right. Who runs the world? We are the masters at multiplication. When a man has clearly articulated his vision, a woman will get under that mission and bring it to life. Because of the nature of femininity, we will take a seed, multiply it, and bring it back full grown. Our problem in submission is when there's nothing for us to receive and to multiply into more.

Can I go deeper with this? Women are the most educated people in the world. Black women in particular are the most educated people in the United States. I say that because as women we are investing in ourselves, we are learning and growing and achieving. No one can come to us and expect us to follow them on the "Cruise to Nowhere." Many of us already have a mission. We had one before our King was even thought of. So, in order for us to submit, Kings have to step up in their Kingdom assignment and give us something to follow. Additionally, marriage is a partnership between equals. We both have individual purpose and destiny, so your King doesn't get to set the mission for your life any more than you get to set the mission for his. You both create a mission for your marriage together.

"Teach A Wife" Tips

Create a mission

So, what do we do with that? How do we communicate in love that we need something to follow? Understanding your own purpose prior to marriage is key. If you look at the garden story in Genesis, before God gave Adam Eve, He gave him work. He gave him purpose. He gave him destiny. No man who is unclear about who he is and what he is called to do is ready to connect himself to anyone else's life. Get your personal mission together first. After you've done that, both of you, then you are able to even consider being in a relationship with anyone else.

As far as creating a marriage mission together, this is where we must have intimate conversations. Can you see why I placed the subject of submission later in the book? We needed to have talked about communication first. Review the wisdom in those sections. It will help you in how you interact with your Beloved around your mission. Remember, it's not often the "what," as it is most certainly the "how."

I'd love to suggest a tool for you that I think will help to broaden this conversation. It's a book by Jimmy Evans called "Mountaintop of Marriage: A Vision Retreat Guidebook." This book will allow you to consider the different areas of spiritual and personal growth, preparation, and vision for your family. It's a practical tool that asks questions and lays out a 12-month planning calendar for you to use and to reference.

It is my opinion that it is not as difficult to submit when you know where you're going. Inherent in women is the need for security. While we know that plans can shift and change, having a plan at all allows us to feel a sense of safety. You need to have a plan, a program for your marriage and life together. The reason why you do it together is because you're talking about two people's lives, not one. You are one, but you are individuals too. Additionally, your joint and individual lives impact the lives of multiplied others.

Your undercover assignment

Lastly, I want to offer you some wisdom that I heard from a talk recently on "Submission and Surrender". Here's what was discussed.

Let's look at the words submission and surrender. Submission, as we said, means "sub-under or below the mission or assignment." In other words, submission is your undercover assignment.

In the next word, surrender, "sur" means "over or above" and render means "to give" or "to deliver." We often look at surrender as "giving up" or as "hands up with a white flag." We see it as giving up our rights. Can we break it apart and put it back together? Surrender can be looked upon as over-delivering or giving above and beyond what's expected.

So let's examine what is so beautiful about these two words when you couple them together and are mindful of their roots. Here is a new way to see "surrender" and "submission."

"You and I are under a God-assigned mission (submission) to give over and above our husband's expectations (surrender) so that he can experience God's love through us."

Back to love

Priceless. It is our undercover assignment to show God's love. It always goes back to love. The truth is, as we stated earlier, it is all about us living out the love of God in us, as us, and through us. We lovingly submit to one another. In submission is also where we see 1 Peter 3 coming to life.

"In the same way, you wives must accept the authority (submit) of your husbands. Then, even if some refuse to obey the Good News, your godly lives will speak to them without any words. They will be won over by observing your pure and reverent lives."

210

It says wives be submitted to your own husbands. May I emphasize husbands, not men? What this passage is saying is that even if your husband is not as spiritual and obedient as you would like him to be, you will win him over because of your life of love and submission to God and in how you pour out love and live submitted to him, your husband. When he sees your godly life, it speaks without any words. You don't need to hit him over the head with the Bible. What they don't need is us preaching at them and telling them what pastor said. Let your life and love preach.

You live the Bible. Live the law of love. Be kind even when he is not. That'll preach louder than any sermon you ever try to play in his hearing. When you take a stand for righteousness in an honorable way and submit to God above all else even if it means you have to tell your husband "No," that makes a statement too. Live in integrity. Submission is not following anyone into foolishness. Let's be clear about that.

From jump

I had to be quite honest with you about the beginning of our relationship. As I said, I just went along to get along. Later, after I had grown up a bit and gotten clearer about submission, there have been definite times in our lives when my husband was making a decision out of fear and I knew it. I took a stand for what was right. I told him as gently as I could that I had to do what it is that God had spoken to me. In those instances, he yielded to me. Again, submission goes both ways because the ultimate submission is to GOD.

Follow the leader

If he had been insistent, he would have to show me where we're going, even if it's by faith, and I would willingly submit and follow him. What we sometimes forget is following presupposes that there is a leader. Position or title does not qualify you to be followed. Leadership does. With authority comes responsibility. Healthy submission requires both parties to do their part.

So, if our husbands want us to follow them, they must lead. When they are not leading, we must be the voice that speaks life to them and let them know that we believe in them and we see them how God sees them so that they will step up. Then, we must give them room and space to do it without simply taking over because of our own fear or impatience.

I do agree that there may sometimes be a decision or action that needs to be made and you may have to just step up and do it. Leadership is something that you share and you do together. The truth is that we should only be following one another as we follow Christ. God is the leader.

Remember the game "Follow the Leader." Oh how we loved that game. As children, we saw it as an honor and pleasure to lead. Everyone had to follow what we were doing and imitate our actions and if they didn't, they were out. Being a leader seemed like a lot of fun. After we grew up, we realized that there was a lot more to it than barking out orders to be followed. Being a leader means that you have to have a vision. You may often be the one that everyone is looking to for direction and to answer all of the questions. There's a lot of pressure in being the leader and carrying the load of the responsibility of it. As we grow up and learn how life really works, we miss those much simpler days of childhood.

Why your husband may not be leading

Sometimes, we are having issues with our husband stepping up to lead because we constantly override him or are not patient enough to allow him the time and space to step up and be the leader. Other times, it could be how critical we have been when he has made mistakes with his decision-making or courses of action. We want a manly man, a masculine man, but we are constantly emasculating him by treating him like a child. We're acting like his mother.

You can be his lover or his mother, but you can't be both.

Stand down Queen. You don't have to control everything. Controlling is often an indication of fear. Trust God and trust in the God in your husband. Share your fears with him. Be vulnerable. Help him to understand. Most of all, let him know that you believe in him and you want him to lead. Then, let him lead. Will you always agree? Nope. Will he make mistakes? Yup. Do you make mistakes too? Absolutely. It will happen, and you will be able to move past it and grow together if you allow your trust and confidence in God and in him to grow.

"Teach A Wife" Tip

As wives and women, we discussed how we have so many roles that we stand in. Even if your husband is very active at home, you probably carry most of the running of your household still. It is a welcome change for me at least to have my husband stand up and take leadership in areas. That is one less thing off of my plate. I'm happy to follow the leader.

To do that, I have to take a deep breath and accept that he will not do everything the way I would. That's fine. I don't have to be bothered with the decisions, and I can release the outcomes to him. I can let go the reins and just go along with his idea and things will work out just fine. I married him because he was a strong, confident, competent man. That has not changed even if he falters from time to time. I falter at times too. Like myself, I invite you to remember why you married your man and to trust in him enough to lead your family together.

What a "Ho" Can Teach A Wife

CHAPTER 17

If Momma (or the Queen Wife) Ain't Happy, Ain't Nobody Happy

Ladies, we are the heart of our homes. We are. We are the ones who set the emotional climate of it. We are physically wired for more emotional processing and connection, and we must maximize that ability. The saying, if Momma, and I'll add the Queen Wife, ain't happy, ain't nobody happy is true. We often set the thermostat, the atmosphere so to speak, of our homes. You can have a beautiful house, but if love isn't between the walls, it will never be a home. If there is not a sense of peace when you step onto the property, you're just walking into a building. This is why your joy and happiness are of most importance. Your mood and your attitude seeps into the lives of not just your husband but also your children. You give them their emotional barometer.

It's on you Boo

It starts with you Queen Wife. Here's the double-edged sword. You and only you are responsible for your happiness. As much as it brings delight to your King to make you happy, it's not his responsibility. As we discussed, he's not really making you happy, he should be adding to your happiness. We should not be looking to them to be the source of our happiness. Our men can contribute to it, but our overall happiness is our choice to make for ourselves, for our marriages and our families.

What? So now they're off the hook more? No. Your King was never on the hook as responsible for your happiness. He is responsible for his own happiness too. The moment that we look to an outside force, person, activity, or event as our source of happiness, we have lost the point. The joy is always in the journey. The satisfaction comes in reaching for more.

You've probably experienced it. You had this big, bodacious goal that you thought would make everything right in your life. You scratched and clawed. You rose and fell. You laughed and cried. You did the hard work. You enjoyed your successes. Finally, you reached your goal. You were on the top of the mountain. The only problem was that it was far less thrilling than you thought it would be. The euphoric feeling of achievement ended much sooner than you wanted it to. You felt like, "Is this all there is to that?"

There is no one person who gets it all right all the time. We are each treasure in earthen vessels. We are all on the Potter's wheel being shaped by the hands of the Master as we spin and twirl, then become dizzy from life at times. It is up to us to find the beauty in every moment. It is our responsibility to see God's hand moving in our lives. We have to attune ourselves to finding humor in even the gravest situations. No one can do that for you. No one can make you have a heart of gratitude. No one can give you the half-full mentality. Being optimistic is a skill that you have to develop. Seeing good in everyone and everything is on you. Contentment is your power play.

"...Godliness with contentment is great gain."
1 Timothy 6:6

Finding contentment

Godliness with contentment is great gain. First and foremost, it is incumbent upon us to walk in our godliness. To find the level of happiness that God created us all to live in, we must see ourselves as god in the Earth. That's who God said that we are. We're made in His image and likeness and put here to rule and to reign, to be fruitful and to multiply—that is to live in abundance. We must see how wonderful and worthy we are. We must allow ourselves to ponder the vastness of God's love for us and the good plans that He has for our lives. We've got to be willing to accept that the road that we are on right now is the perfect place to be in order to create the abundant life that God has for us.

When we understand and accept that God is still on the throne and He's asking us to rise to our own thrones, everything is all good. It doesn't matter what state you are in, it's still good. God is still using every circumstance for your good. It may be a subtle shift for you or it may be a seismic shift to embrace that, but when you know that no matter what happens is working out for your good, the bad doesn't seem as bad anymore.

"And we know that all things work together for good to those who love God, to those who are the called according to His purpose."
Romans 8:28

This mindset allows us to be content. When our communication with our Kings is on point, we choose to be happy, and even if it's a disaster right now, we still choose to be happy. We make it our aim to find things in our lives that are good. We tune our dials, our emotional dials, onto what feels good right now. We place all of my attention on

217

what's working. We are content. It's our power play because it involves faith. Are you willing to call those things that be not as though they were? Will you act as if? Can you look at your man when he's acting like a lunatic and still treat him like a King because you know it will call him higher?

See this is the grown folks' stuff. This is the stuff that the women with full gray heads will tell you. They will tell you that they had to look at their husbands who were acting like plum fools through God's eyes and still call the King forth. We don't like that. We like to look at what we see with our natural eyes and say what we see. We feel secure in that. We want confirmation from our senses. That's not faith. And the Scripture says that the just will live by faith. Queen Wives, it's our time to go higher.

The realm of faith is where the great gain comes in. When you and I can simply focus on creating the God kind of life in ourselves and with ourselves, that level of peace, ease, and grace create such rich soil for blessings to grow in. This level of belief sets the ground of our hearts to be ready to receive the seeds that God is continually planting in our lives and to nurture those that are growing from deep within.

Our trust in God roots and grounds us so that when the storms of life come, we might bend but we will never break. I have to tell it to you straight up. It's the only way I know how to be. If you are dependent upon how your husband looks, acts, or feels in order to be happy with yourself or in your marriage, you're in trouble.

I had to come to a point where I made my own happiness a priority. I had to discover what made me happy. I had to create space and time to engage in whatever states or activities that entailed. I had to be okay with saying No to everyone else and Yes to myself. Is that selfish? It could be, but in this case it really is not. It is impossible for you to have a happy marriage without first having a happy life.

The Proverbs 31 Wife

"10 Who can find a virtuous wife? For her worth is far above rubies.

11 The heart of her husband safely trusts her; So he will have no lack of gain.

12 She does him good and not evil All the days of her life.

13 She seeks wool and flax, And willingly works with her hands.

14 She is like the merchant ships, She brings her food from afar.

15 She also rises while it is yet night, And provides food for her household, and a portion for her maidservants.

16 She considers a field and buys it; From her profits she plants a vineyard.

17 She girds herself with strength, and strengthens her arms.

18 She perceives that her merchandise is good, and her lamp does not go out by night.

19 She stretches out her hands to the distaff, and her hand holds the spindle.

20 She extends her hand to the poor, Yes, she reaches out her hands to the needy.

21 She is not afraid of snow for her household, For all her household is clothed with scarlet.

22 She makes tapestry for herself; Her clothing is fine linen and purple.

23 Her husband is known in the gates, When he sits among the elders of the land.

24 She makes linen garments and sells them, And supplies sashes for the merchants.

25 Strength and honor are her clothing; She shall rejoice in time to come.

26 She opens her mouth with wisdom, And on her tongue is the law of kindness.

27 She watches over the ways of her household, And does not eat the bread of idleness.

28 Her children rise up and call her blessed; Her husband also, and he praises her:

29 "Many daughters have done well, But you excel them all."

30 Charm is deceitful and beauty is passing, But a woman who fears the Lord, she shall be praised.

31 Give her of the fruit of her hands, And let her own works praise her in the gates."

Proverbs 31:10-31

Know your worth

Look at the Proverbs 31 wife. It says in v.10, "Who can find a virtuous and capable woman or wife? She is more precious than rubies." It is asking, who can find a strong, capable, wealthy wife? Where are the women who are strong enough to deal with their Kings' weaknesses? The Sisters who will look at their falling and failings but still see them in their strengths? Where are the wives who are willing to tap into all of their vast capabilities without allowing fear to stop them? Those who will confront every lie that's keeping them from rising? Where are the Queens who know their worth and value and the assets that they bring to every situation? Where is she? She is more precious than rubies. That means that she is rare. Diamonds may be a girl's best friend, but rubies are actually rarer and more valuable than diamonds. This Queen Wife stands head and shoulders above the crowd. Is that you? When you know your worth and understand the presence that you bring to every situation, it creates a space for joy to abide in. When your happiness is not dependent on any other person, that's power.

Can he trust you?

Queen, can your husband safely trust in you? Are you secure enough in yourself that he knows he can rely on you? Or are you scattered, here and there and everywhere and unstable? Is his heart safe in your hands? Is his name safe in your mouth? Are you woman enough to face the past and move forward, or are you constantly holding him down to a past version of himself? Do you keep your struggles between the two of you and perhaps a prayer partner or is all your business out in the streets? Can he trust you? Will all of his failures be broadcasted to all of your friends?

A wise woman builds her house and a foolish woman tears it down with her own hands. Be honest. Are you tearing down your house yourself? Are you tearing your man down with your words or your sneering glares? Are you emasculating him and treating him like a child? Have you lost respect for him? Trust me, he can sense it. He can feel it. What are you going to do about it?

You are going to have to ask him what it would take to rebuild trust with you if trust has been compromised. You will have to identify where he has felt that you have not done well by him. It's time to eat a little humble pie. Ask and then just listen. Don't refute it. Don't try to explain it. Just listen. Accept his point of view even if you don't agree with it. Have another conversation if you feel that you need to clarify something, but let him get it out. If there is no trust, there is no happy marriage.

Besides, it feels good to be trusted. You know when someone believes in you and can rely on you. That's a good feeling. You have to see yourself as trustworthy first. Do you trust yourself? Can you believe your own word? Rebuild trust with yourself and then work it out with Hubby too.

Do your thing

As Proverbs 31 Wives, we must find happiness in ourselves and in our own roles in life. As keepers of the heart and happiness of our homes, we've got to do our own thing. We set the happiness index when we get our whole lives. When you are constantly putting everyone before yourself and then leaving little or no time for yourself, your own happiness suffers. This woman had a lot going on. I would argue that these were pictures of different seasons in her life as opposed to all of these things going on at once, but you get the feeling that she was a boss. She was handling her business and living her life but taking care of her family too.

That may not be popular today with all the "me only focus" society and the competition that is bred out there between men and women, as if we need to compete with men. We don't. Men cannot do what we do. Know your power Queen. All of mankind came through a woman. We carry the seeds of the world. We incubate them. We cause them to be more. Conversely, we may think that we can do what our men do because so many men have been absent in our lives and we just had to make do any way that we could. That is not true. We cannot do all that they do either.

I love our Kings, but I am so happy that I am a woman. I love who we are and how we are made. The strength that we represent. I love the ability that we have to transform. I'm happy with my womanhood. I see it as a distinct advantage. Do you? Are you happy to be a woman?

"And the Lord God said, It is not good that the man should be alone; I will make him an help meet for him."
Genesis 2:18

Happy to help

I am happy to help. We all know the creation story in Genesis. God made all of the Earth and then He made mankind. He placed Adam in the garden, gave him some work to do, and then stated that it was not good that man should be alone. You might also state that as all one. There's a difference between being alone and being lonely. Adam had God so he was never alone, but what he didn't have was someone just like him to walk alongside of him.

Enter Eve. And, a grand entrance it was. So let's go back. God made the heavens and the Earth and everything in it; and He said that it was not just good, it was very good. What wasn't very good was that Adam was the only one like him on the Earth. I believe that Genesis says that God made mankind, not just man as in Adam. He made all of us when he made one of us. In other words, Adam was pregnant with Eve for lack of a better term. God put him to sleep, took a rib out, and specially fashioned this woman's body around it. As for her purpose, she is just as called, anointed, and appointed. One area that she is especially gifted in is in being a help meet for Adam.

Stay with me. I'm fixing it up for you Queen. A helper? For a lot of us, helper might mean that you aren't the main one. You aren't in charge. You're just an afterthought. You come just to help out whoever has the most important role and is really running things. This could not be farther from the truth. Being a helper puts us in pretty good company. John 14:26 calls the Holy Spirit the Helper. It's the Holy Spirit who teaches us in all things. It's the Holy Spirit who brings all things to our remembrance, reminding us of who we are and what God has spoken to us. It's the Holy Spirit who hovers over the face of the deep in the beginning and creates. Come on now helpers! We are the manifestors. We are the ones who bring things forth. We have great power woman of God!

I'm happy to help. Let's go deeper! Oftentimes when we see the term "help meet" it is explained as help that is suitable or help that is compatible. It's more than that. If you look at it in its original text, you will see something that is very different. Help meet is derived from two words: "ezer" and "kenegdo." When we are interpreting Scripture, it is very important to look at the original Hebrew or Greek because sometimes the words in our language can mean or imply something very different. What is commonly translated as help actually means help and so much more. It also means "to rescue" or "to save." It means that we are often the instrument that God will use to save or rescue our husbands in ways. Interesting. "Kenegdo" is only listed once in Genesis. Because of that, we don't have other references to compare it with. It is often translated as "meet" or "fit for." If you break the roots of that word down, it can also be translated as "in front of" or "opposite of" or "exactly corresponding to." It is similar to when you look in a mirror and you face yourself. As Eve, we were not designed to be exactly like Adam. We were designed to be his mirror opposite. We were designed to possess the qualities, the capabilities, and the attributes that our husbands lack. Another quick look at our physiology confirms that. We were designed to fit together so that in our coming together we create life. Did you catch that? When you come together spiritually, mentally, emotionally, and physically, you create life.

Be happy to help. You are your King's complete spiritual equal in life with a saving power that complements him and his needs, and he does the same for you. This is your place of power Queen. He needs you to add the significant pieces that he lacks. The opposite is also true. He complements your needs too.

Be supported

I read something recently that I really liked. A husband is to be the "band of the house." Many times, we can feel unsupported. We feel like we have so much to do and that there is no one to take the load off of us. Allow your husband to be the band of your house. I see that as meaning that he should create a container to hold it all together with his masculine constancy and strength so that within the container, we can create and multiply and make our home and lives a haven of beauty and happiness for each other and our families. Now, this resting on God and in our Kings is difficult to do if you personally are not happy. Let's explore a few tips to help you expand in happiness.

"Teach A Wife" Tips

Get your Queen Wife Journal.

I invite you to consider these.

1. Are you happy with yourself? If not, why not? What's going on in your mind and heart that is preventing this? I'll suggest my own book here, "Queen Arise." It is part of my own journey into deeper self-love, acceptance, and forgiveness, and letting go of the past so that I could stand in my power, the truth of who I am as a Queen and be happy with myself. It can do the same for you too. To get a signed copy directly from me, go to www.queenarisebook.com. Outside of the U.S., get your coy at bit.ly/queenarise40.

2. What things can you do to be happier? That will vary. Forgive your bad decisions. Let go of your abusive childhood. Go on trips by yourself, with your Hubby, your family or with friends. Create your physical intimacy with your King. Release excess weight internally and externally. Take up a new hobby that you haven't created time for in the past. Spend a whole day each month getting pampered from head to toe (That's mine!).

3. How can you create a happier, freer atmosphere in your marriage? Go on Date Night. Celebrate the first time that you met? Your engagement? Your anniversary? Connect with other couples? Join a co-ed sports league: bowling, softball, tennis, etc. How can you incorporate more fun?

4. What's one thing you can do or at least start within 24 hours to

225

make your home a more peaceful, happy haven? Have a family game night. Break out the Uno cards or Spades and play as teams. Do a potluck with your extended family. Have movie night.

Think about these things. Add to the list. Allow God to speak to you. It's our divine right to have and enjoy life to the full until it overflows. May joy be your portion.

Queen Wife Mastery

Some final words

Wow! Let me applaud you for starting and finishing this book. The truth is, the journey is really just beginning. I know, really know that God is doing a new thing in you and in your marriage. I have prayed for you earnestly, that your faith fail not.

In this book, I have really only scratched the surface. There is so much more that I could share with you. That is why I offer the Queen Wife Mastery Membership Program. You can get information on it at www.teachawife.com.

I'd like to ask you a question...

What would it feel like for you to have a marriage that is passionate and peaceful, where you love and respect, honor and accept each other? How would it feel to have intimacy, real intimacy—spiritually, emotionally, and sexually—that satisfies you both? Not only is it possible, it's what God intended. By now, I think you also believe that marriage is supposed to be a delight. It's supposed to be fun. Do you agree? We are supposed to have a marriage made in heaven that we live out on Earth. It really is our divine birthright.

As you saw, I was struggling so desperately in my marriage.

Now, I support women all over the world to get to their hot, holy & happily ever after too. We've been married for almost 22 years. But, since you read the book, you know that most of those 22 years being married felt like a ball and chain, like doing time.

I've never been in jail, but I felt like I was in a prison.

To say that our communication was less than desirable was an understatement. We had issues with trust and vulnerability. It didn't feel safe to share. Let's not even talk about money. And then sex?? We're married, right? We're supposed to be having sex. It felt like we were just roommates with occasional benefits.

One day, I just reached the end of my rope. You know things happen when a woman gets tired of being tired and makes up her mind that change is happening now. Are you ready to make up your mind? I said this is it. I did NOT give the younger part of my youth up for this. That's it. I am going to enjoy my life. I am going to be happy. I am going to have a happy marriage. I will do everything I can do to get there.

I began to study and learn and grow and work on myself. My husband saw the changes and he began to change too. Sometimes we are looking for our spouse to change. Why do I have to do this work? Remember, Emerson Eggerichs, author of "Love and Respect," puts it this way. "Let the more mature one step up?" I had to woman up. Put my big girl panties on. And, here we are. Happy!

You shouldn't have to suffer year after year without relief. You should not have to numb yourself out ignoring one another or shopping or throwing your whole life into your children, just going along to get along year after year because the happy marriage you thought you'd have is not happening.

You are not alone!

Also, you shouldn't have to go it alone. God's desire is for us to have and enjoy life to the full until it overflows. I call it the John 10:10 life, the Divine Life. Do you believe that includes your marriage? Marriage is honorable. It is to be a place of love, joy, peace, and passion. It's a place where we can be ourselves and be accepted. It's a place of growth and transformation. It's also a place of joy and happiness.

You deserve that.

To check out the Queen Wife Mastery Membership Program go to www.teachawife.com.

I have developed the Queen Wife Mastery Membership as a monthly online membership where I will share with you the spiritual truths and practical wisdom I have learned to finally, really love my marriage. In this membership, you will...

**discover your true value as a Queen Wife and how God has called you to live in partnership and power together

**Deepen your spiritual intimacy with God and your husband so you can achieve the oneness God intended

**learn how to deal with conflicts without crushing one another and how to communicate with love and respect

**learn how to fan the flames of your love and rekindle your sexual intimacy and romance even if it seems that the fire has gone out

**discover what really motivates your husband to change without manipulation of any kind

**identify how to deal with the kids, your in-laws and outlaws so you can successfully manage any family pressures together

**learn how to allow your husband to lead, to bring out the King in him, and how to inspire him to lovingly take care of you

**and SO, so much more!

Why monthly? Why am I doing this?

Because every month, you're married. I don't know about you, but in the past, my husband and I would have a big conflict, we'd fight, argue, and then and we'd work on it. Things would get better and honestly, we'd chill. It wasn't long before something else crept up because we weren't paying attention to our relationship and sustaining the changes.

It's almost like you're flooring it down the highway, flying, going 80 mph. If you take your foot off the gas, eventually your car slows down and stops, right? That's what was happening with our marriage. Starts and stops. I'm going to help you to keep going on the highway of happiness with relationship with sustained speed in the right direction by giving you a theme each month to work on to improve your marriage, so you can keep your positive momentum going. Is that good?

To get all of the details of the Queen Wife Mastery Membership Program, go to www.teachawife.com.

For one-on-one mentoring and coaching or to book me as a speaker for your next event or conference, please direct all inquiries to support@ queensforchrist.org.

Thank you for going on this journey. Praying for your expanding happiness,

Queen Karin